# The
# Brain
# Fitness
# Puzzle
# Book

**Dr Gareth Moore B.Sc (Hons) M.Phil Ph.D**
is the internationally bestselling author of a wide
range of brain-training and puzzle books for both
children and adults, including *Enigma: Crack the
Code*, *Ultimate Dot to Dot*, *Brain Games for Clever
Kids*, *Lateral Logic* and *Extreme Mazes*. His books
have sold millions of copies in the UK alone,
and have been published in over thirty different
languages. He is also the creator of online brain-
training site BrainedUp.com, and runs the daily
puzzle site PuzzleMix.com.

Find him online at DrGarethMoore.com.


**Dr Helena Gellersen** obtained her doctorate in
psychology from the University of Cambridge
studying the cognitive neuroscience of memory
in ageing. She now holds a postdoctoral position
at the German Center for Neurodegenerative
Diseases researching brain changes in preclinical
Alzheimer's disease and developing novel memory
tasks to aid in its early detection. Her research has
been featured in multiple peer-reviewed journals,
podcasts and blogs. Together with Dr Gareth
Moore she co-authored the puzzle book *Memory
Palace Master* in which she guides the reader
through the cognitive neuroscience of memory and
explains mnemonic strategies.

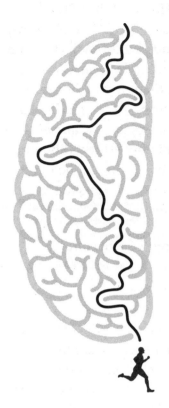

# The Brain Fitness Puzzle Book

## DR GARETH MOORE
## DR HELENA M. GELLERSEN

Michael O'Mara Books Limited

First published in Great Britain in 2023 by
Michael O'Mara Books Limited
9 Lion Yard
Tremadoc Road
London SW4 7NQ

A CIP catalogue record for this book is available from the British Library.

Papers used by Michael O'Mara Books Limited are natural, recyclable products made
from wood grown in sustainable forests. The manufacturing processes conform to the
environmental regulations of the country of origin.

ISBN: 978-1-78929-457-6 in paperback print format

1 2 3 4 5 6 7 8 9 10

Designed and typeset by Gareth Moore
Includes images from Shutterstock.com

Printed and bound by CPI Group (UK) Ltd, Croydon, CR0 4YY

www.mombooks.com

MIX
Paper | Supporting
responsible forestry
FSC
www.fsc.org
FSC® C171272

# Contents

To all who helped me along the path
to becoming a scientist and most of
all to my family and Andrea.
I can't thank you enough!


*– Helena M. Gellersen*

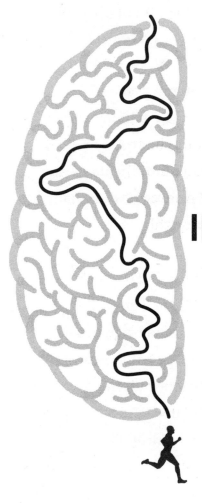

# INTRODUCTION

# Introduction

Humans have a remarkable capacity to learn, imagine and reason, which has allowed our species to evolve from the first attempts to wield fire to the creation of the nuclear bomb within 300,000 years. To put that into perspective: if the Earth's age was compressed from its 4.6 billion years to just twenty-four hours, humans would not have made it onto the scene until the last ninety seconds of the day – an impressively short period of time to become the dominant species on the planet.

The key to this success is that 1.5 kg fatty organ which uses up to twenty per cent of the body's total energy consumption: the brain. The average human brain has about eighty-six billion neurons, which exchange trillions of signals with each other every second. Neuroscience is only starting to uncover how it is that the human brain can produce feats of art and science which shape our cultural history and our understanding of the world. Much remains which scientists do not understand yet. What is clear, though, is that learning, creative thinking and reasoning are inherently human, meaning that every one of us has the basic machinery required for these abilities. Even better: you can learn how to use this machinery more effectively.

## Where will this take me?

In this book, you will read about the basics of the brain and key players in human cognition which keep us going in our endeavours to remember, learn, solve problems and think creatively. You will take it from theory to practice as you tackle increasingly more challenging puzzles that cover a variety of cognitive functions.

Before you embark on this journey, it is important to keep in mind that science cannot offer a magic wand you can wave or a spell book that will teach you how to 'boost your brain power'. Just as your body gets gradually stronger as you put in the time to go for a run or lift weights, your brain also needs time to change. Completing mental exercises will not transform you into the new Einstein. But what science can do is use the knowledge of how the human brain gives rise to its various cognitive functions to help you add to the repertoire of strategies you can use to complete these exercises more efficiently and carry your knowledge into everyday life.

## Why should I care?

Physical health has long been in the focus of health professionals and the general public. Brain health has only become a hot topic more recently. Of course, these two concepts are linked with one another: what is good for your

muscles, your cardiovascular system and your gut is also good for your brain – it's all connected, after all. There are some exercises, though, that might not make you sweat in the literal sense, but which are just the right flavour for your brain. Keeping cognitively active and challenging yourself with new tasks and experiences is at the core of a healthy brain. You can therefore view this book as one part of a toolkit you may want to keep handy when you feel like it's time for some mental exercise and when you seek to learn more about the organ that holds the secrets to your memories, your intelligence and your creativity.

Although learning has the ultimate goal of acquiring new knowledge and skills, thereby improving upon your existing capabilities, when done right it also provides other powerful psychological benefits. You may have heard that physical exercise can release biochemicals that improve mood and reduce stress. Intriguingly, though, you may not have to don your gym clothes to achieve similar effects. Mental exercises and learning can also be deeply satisfying when you are provided with engaging challenges, such as the puzzles presented in this book.

Humans are naturally curious, and this curiosity has been vital for our survival and evolution. It drove us to venture

into new territory, discover new species of plants and animals, test the boundaries of our abilities and devise new uses for the materials found around us. Without the need for discovery and a hunger for learning, we would have never come to where we are today. The journey of learning can therefore serve as its own reward.

## A varied practice

Similar to any physical exercise, variety is also key for mental exercises. Completing a thousand sudoku or hundreds of crossword puzzles may be fun and relaxing – and there is nothing wrong with that, of course – but if you are looking for a little more, then getting out of your comfort zone is crucial. Although your brain is inherently curious, on the other hand it also gets lazy. Just as our curiosity had an important evolutionary benefit, you may be surprised to hear that this 'laziness' is actually reflective of a different powerful evolutionary mechanism: the brain's ability to establish routines which minimize the amount of effort needed to go about your day.

Completing the same, familiar exercise is comfortable – you know what to expect, you know what to do and you know that you will succeed. If you're a sudoku pro or a crossword mastermind, this positive expectation means

that you are pretty certain that completing the exercise will feel rewarding. You are essentially exploiting your existing cognitive resources. This is great when you begin a new exercise session because it will get you settled in. However, the mental energy expended on a familiar task may be minimal and the brain is not required to develop new resources and learn new strategies that will allow you to expand your knowledge and skills. This is where the benefit of exploring tasks with novel demands comes in, even if it may feel daunting to begin with.

This choice between exploration, or curiosity-driven behaviour, and exploitation, or the tendency to choose a safer bet, is ubiquitous in everyday life. Just think about the last time you went to your favourite restaurant and had to decide whether you would go with your tried-and-tested usual or a new option on the menu. So, if you are confronted with particularly challenging tasks that may feel discouraging as you work your way through this book, remember that you are pushing your brain to explore, which is ultimately the key to expanding your resources and getting you out of a routine.

## The cognitive battery

Most things in life are fleeting: the words spoken to you by a friend during a dinner conversation, the images flickering before you while watching a movie – they are here in an instant and then they are gone. But we need to hold on to them in order to keep track of the conversation with our friend, the plot of the movie, or this very sentence. Otherwise, we would entirely lack any sense of context and would perpetually find ourselves in a state of confusion.

The first challenge for your brain is therefore to retain information even after it is no longer immediately present in the environment. However, not everything we see, hear or smell is relevant at a given point in time. When you are focusing on the conversation with your friend, you don't need to hear what the couple at the neighbouring table is arguing about (even if it may feel tempting to listen in).

Another challenge for your brain is to block out the kinds of distractions that are not crucial for the task at hand, while also making sure that you are still capable of responding to other potentially important information, for instance when your phone rings unexpectedly or another friend happens to pass by and calls out your name. This rather complex feat requires cognitive flexibility to direct your limited attentional

capacities to relevant information and adapt quickly to new task demands.

These functions form the bedrock for many complex cognitive tasks, as you will see later. One type of puzzle you will encounter in this book is therefore geared towards teaching you strategies to retain more information in your short-term memory and use it flexibly to solve complex problems.

Vision is the sense humans rely on most and we have a dedicated short-term memory system for visuospatial stimuli which is separate from that in which we store verbal information. This system helps us to form correct internal representations of objects and their relationships, which helps us to manipulate the world around us to fit our needs. One popular exercise of this type of task is the Rubik's cube, in which differently coloured square elements of a cube have to be moved around as to assign all squares of the same colour to one specific side of the cube. While you may not break the speed record in a Rubik's cube competition after reading this book, the puzzles of visuospatial cognition will challenge you to better manipulate visual information in your mind's eye.

Besides short-term memory, your brain also has long-term memory systems which ensure that information you experience in your environment can be recalled at a later time, enabling you to remember that dinner conversation the next time you catch up with your friend, bringing to mind cherished moments of your last holiday, reciting the lyrics to your favourite song or acing an exam. There are strategies that can help you increase the likelihood of making newly learned information available to you at a later time and in this book you will get the opportunity to try your hand at some of them.

The most high-level cognitive functions of which humans are capable involve creativity and reasoning. These abilities have given rise to humankind's greatest accomplishments: art and culture which have endured for centuries and in some cases even millennia; inventions of novel technologies which allow us to shape the world around us; and great discoveries leading us to a deeper understanding of the universe, be it of planets light years in the distance or the organ that allows you to comprehend this very sentence. Becoming the new da Vinci requires a lifetime of disciplined study (in addition to what was likely an unfair genetic advantage). But honing your creative and logical thinking skills can be done one step at a time by learning more about the processes that support

you in solving complex problems and avoiding common pitfalls.

## Your journey

Finally, after any intense physical exercise, ending with a restorative stretch and a cool-down is essential. For your mental exercises, finishing with some simpler puzzles will keep you from getting too discouraged if the higher difficulty exercises were frustrating at times and if you found it difficult to progress.

In this book, you can test yourself on a variety of cognitive skills, including exercises that tax your memory, your mental flexibility, your visuospatial skills, your reasoning and your creative thinking. That way, you are guaranteed to be faced with novel challenges at each turn of a page, giving you the opportunity to benefit from a wide variety of exercises. It also gives you an understanding of where your strengths lie and where you would benefit most from focusing your attention when attempting new puzzles.

The book is structured in a manner that imitates a physical exercise session, with a warm-up, a ramping up phase, a high intensity 'cardio' challenge and a cool-down. No exercise begins with the heaviest weights or the fastest

sprint. Similarly, when taking on the puzzles in this book and trying your hand at new strategies, you may first want to get in the groove with something light to warm up. You can comfortably begin with some puzzles that will be quite familiar to you, that get your creative juices flowing and prepare you for the next level. You will gradually be introduced to more challenging puzzles that build on your learning from previous sections. You will also read about strategies that you can employ to become more proficient at the exercises.

## Mix it up

Throughout this whole journey, keep your own pace and develop your own structure of how you want to approach these tasks. If on a given day you prefer to keep it light, go with some warm-up exercises and a few puzzles from the second difficulty level. If you feel like it's time for a challenge, work your way up with a warm-up and then jump to the high-intensity puzzles. After all, learning is meant to be fun and rewarding, yet challenging in just the right way without becoming discouraging. In order to keep you motivated and keep track of your progress, each puzzle will award you with a particular number of points, depending on how successfully you complete the exercise – see **'Track your points' on page 192** for further information. You can

note the number of points you collected per page by using the boxes at the top of the relevant pages, so you can then look back and compare your achievements on subsequent sessions.

## Pesky habits

It's hard to shake a habit, and it can be just as hard to establish new ones. Anyone who ever started a diet, a new workout regime, or a new book can attest to that. If some habits are detrimental and keep us from achieving our goals, why would nature ever devise such a seemingly flawed system? It's easy. Habits are efficient because they don't require many cognitive resources, meaning you don't have to think much. When you're trying to quit junk food, that's bad news because your brain will automatically send you on your way to the ice cream in your freezer.

Ironically, when your goal is to learn something new that automatization is exactly what you want. Cognitive training is meant to establish new routines that allow you to solve problems more efficiently. That efficiency is best supported when you have internalized strategies, automated the cognitive machinery needed to solve the task and, as a result, increased processing speed for similar tasks. The automatic craving for that ice cream is the price for the effortless use of

language and ease of basic arithmetic in your mind. When you're trying to break or make a habit, it's helpful to change your environment in a way that makes it harder to follow it (placing the jar of cookies at the top shelf) or a lot easier to get going (have your workout clothes or puzzle book ready and in reach when you wake up – that is if you're a morning person).

To help you form a routine for your cognitive training, you could develop a strategy for how you want to work through this book: do you want to make clear progress and follow a strict regime, or do you prefer to take it easy? Do you set yourself a certain amount of time aside every day? Is there a certain time of the day you want to define as your dedicated puzzle time? There is, of course, nothing wrong with going with the flow and deciding spontaneously – it all depends on what you hope to achieve. Nonetheless, studies have shown that for both physical and mental exercises setting yourself a specific goal and schedule at the get-go can help to keep you going in the longer term. So does rewarding yourself after you have completed your exercises. But make sure that the reward does not hugely outweigh the mental effort you exerted to complete the puzzles. One TV episode for a completed sudoku, memory or reasoning puzzle may be a bit too generous.

## What else can I do to support brain health?

There are many building blocks to a healthy brain, giving you plenty of means to take your health into your own hands. Here is a reminder about the best scientifically proven steps you can take to help maintain and even improve cognitive function.

The first tool in your arsenal is what you are holding now: a means to promote lifelong learning and cognitive engagement. As you know by now, novelty and diverse experiences keep your brain from sliding into that lazy routine. For instance, it has been shown that occupations which require managing people, analysing data, operating complex machinery, or taking on different projects with varying requirements already provide substantial benefits by providing new challenges day by day. For those already enjoying retirement, it is therefore important to replace such experiences with other means of challenging your brain. Excellent leisure time examples are acquiring a new language, playing musical instruments, engaging in other forms of artistic pastimes, or taking up a hobby that requires you to learn new motor skills, such as dancing, tennis or golf.

Physical activity and diet are of course the most frequently cited behaviours supporting health, and with good reason. Exercise improves heart, lung and muscle functions, benefits memory and cognitive abilities, promotes the growth of new blood vessels in the brain and even results in the birth of new neurons in some brain regions. But you don't have to start practising for a marathon just yet. Although high-intensity exercise is most effective to promote these positive effects on the brain, even a half-hour walk brings benefits over prolonged sitting. A varied diet full of vitamin-rich fruit and vegetables and healthy fats such as those contained in nuts, certain types of oils and fish, also forms the basis of a healthy body and brain.

In contrast, you may be surprised to hear that social engagement is similarly important as a healthy behaviour. It seems so simple, yet maintaining a social network and interacting with different people is actually a rather complex task for the brain as it involves exposure to novelty and the processing and memorization of information about many individuals and their relationships. Even more importantly, social engagement protects people from experiencing loneliness, one of the most detrimental factors to both our mental and cognitive health given the deep-rooted human need for connection and belonging.

Finally, good sleep is essential in keeping us healthy, with most people requiring about seven to eight hours every night. Much about the role of sleep is still an enigma, but what we do know is that during sleep our brain promotes the formation of permanent new connections between brain cells necessary for learning, a process termed 'neuronal plasticity' and believed by scientists to be one of the reasons why newborns spend most of their time sleeping. Severe sleep deprivation can be deadly, and a chronic lack of sleep or poor sleep quality will not only affect your mood and energy levels, it will also slow down your brain, impede the formation of new memories and increase your risk of cognitive decline. Ultimately, poor sleep will make it more difficult for you to bring yourself to exercise or make the effort to eat healthily. It will also make it less likely that you will reap the benefits from completing the puzzles in this book.

You see, there is no such thing as the holy grail for a healthy brain. Rather, a 'fit' brain is a mosaic comprised of multiple smaller pieces. The more of these healthy behaviours you engage in, the better, but of course it is not always easy to tick every box. Most people juggle many responsibilities, be it their education, their jobs, or caring for children or relatives, and if we stress ourselves about adhering to all the health

advice that we may be bombarded with, this will in itself be detrimental to our health, as it can create anxiety. Take the steps that you can and gradually but continuously begin to work on incorporating others. As you know, building new habits is difficult and if you hope to see lasting changes, small moments of accomplishment will get you further than large expectations of immediate life-changing effects, which may ultimately leave you disappointed and make you more likely to quit. That goes for both the puzzles in this book and the other health behaviours described here.

You have now already learned quite a bit about the basics of a healthy brain and key cognitive functions, but you are only getting started. So, let's dive into the actual practice and begin your puzzle journey...

**Good luck!**

**Dr Helena Gellersen**

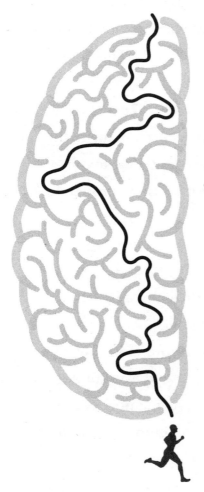

# 1.

# WARMING

# UP

## *Warming up*

Taking on new challenges can be daunting. We will start slowly and then gradually increase the difficulty of the exercises to get you in the right groove. In this chapter, you will be introduced to some basic concepts of how the brain supports core cognitive functions and you will get to try your hand at a variety of puzzles geared to tax each of them. But before you start, you may want to take some time to think about what you hope to get out of your journey through this book.

## A good team

In any good team diversity, effective division of labour, and communication are essential. After all, you want to create synergy between the members of your team. Yet, at the same time, it is also important to avoid everything crashing down like a house of cards if one member of the team underperforms, is injured, or leaves entirely. The same goes for your means of communication. To be more robust, there needs to be both flexibility and a degree of redundancy in terms of skills among your team members and possible communication channels. The brain manages to balance these needs quite well: although certain regions are specialists for particular cognitive functions such as vision, hearing, planning, and laying down new memories, they don't work

alone and cells can rewire themselves and take up the jobs of their neighbours to some extent. That's why in the course of Alzheimer's disease neurodegeneration can occur before a person notices cognitive decline.

Once we have reached adulthood, most brain regions cease to generate new neurons. In adults, it is therefore not so much the number of new neurons that reflects how much we can or have learned. The tree-shaped neurons are already settled comfortably within their forest of cells and they won't go anywhere. Rather, what is altered are the branch-like appendages with which the cell stretches towards its neighbours to pass along information. Learning can result in the formation of new or altered connections between cells and brain regions. You can liken this to your team of neurons becoming better at processing information and communicating more successfully with one another to master a task.

These changes are what researchers refer to as 'brain plasticity', which is our remarkable capacity for learning that we maintain even into older age. It's also why it is possible to bounce back from cognitive defects observed right after a traumatic brain injury or a stroke. Ultimately, the goal you will be pursuing as you work through this book is forming

new connections and making them last, reflecting your improved skills and acquired knowledge. So, while your grey matter may not be able to go for a run, the cells within it sure can move to form new branches and therefore new connections.

Now, let's meet the members of your team that you will send through the exercises in this book.

## Your note taker – short-term memory

Simply seeing our environment is not enough to guide our actions. Visuospatial information, speech, taste and smell can disappear quickly from our surroundings and, to act on them, we need some form of representation even after their physical presence has ceased. Our brain has dedicated short-term memory storage mechanisms that act as a buffer to keep in mind information we just experienced even after it has disappeared from our immediate environment. Rather than letting it slip away like sand through a sieve, the brain regions that process auditory input can maintain something akin to an echo of this information, while the brain regions responsible for vision do the same with visual stimuli. However, these echoes are extremely vulnerable and fade away quickly if they are not immediately relevant to our actions and if we do not focus our attention to hold on to

them. Essentially, your short-term storage can be likened to a note taker in class who only has a blackboard available to jot down the flood of new information with which the teacher of life is bombarding him or her. Once the whole board is full, the note taker needs to wipe the board to keep up – and not everything that was written there in the first instance will be recalled later. There is simply too much interference from subsequent stimuli which degrade the contents of your buffer.

In its most basic form, short-term memory will simply hold information in mind just as you originally experienced it. You can practice doing so in the following puzzle.

# 1.1: Digit memorization

Read the first set of digits below just once through. Then, cover this page and rewrite the digits as accurately as you can on the opposite page. Once done, repeat with each set on this page in turn until you find you can no longer repeat the set of digits correctly. This will give you an idea of the natural limits of your short-term memory.

**Test 1**

## 8 2 7 4 3 7

**Test 2**

## 7 3 5 1 2 4 5

**Test 3**

## 4 0 9 2 4 3 0 1

**Test 4**

## 8 1 4 0 5 2 6 3 9

**Test 5**

## 3 6 4 1 5 8 2 4 7 2

**Test 6**

## 5 9 3 1 8 2 0 7 3 6 4

# *Digit recall*

**Test 1**

........................................................................................................................

**Test 2**

........................................................................................................................

**Test 3**

........................................................................................................................

**Test 4**

........................................................................................................................

**Test 5**

........................................................................................................................

**Test 6**

........................................................................................................................

## Your architect – working memory and executive functions

As you go through life you don't just need to keep an echo or reflection of the stimuli around you in mind. You also need to use these representations to plan your actions and make decisions. This is where 'note taking' on its own is not sufficient, where you are required to manipulate the contents of your short-term memory to meet a goal. Researchers have termed this active manipulation of our short-term storage 'working memory'. It's short-term memory in action.

Working memory belongs to a set of processes that control and guide our thoughts and actions: executive functions – the architect of cognition. They take the building blocks contained in your short-term memory store, plan steps to achieve a goal defined by the task at hand, help in the active search of your long-term memory to find the knowledge needed to complete that task, inhibit alternative, unsuitable options, monitor your progress as you inch closer to your goal and update your status as you work your way through a problem.

Sounds complicated and abstract? Let's take a look at puzzle '1.2: Country confusion' on page 34 in which you are presented with words, the letters of which have to be

rearranged to form names of countries. The visual short-term memory representations need to be actively manipulated to move around the individual elements. This is still rather simple for the first word: few letters need to be kept in mind, there are few possible solutions. But it becomes more challenging as the words become longer: more elements need to be remembered, more potential options need to be retrieved from long-term memory and incorrect ones need to be put aside, and you need to be more careful to make sure you are not missing any letters. The puzzles in this book will largely focus on working memory to train not only your short-term store but also your cognitive flexibility.

## 1.2: Country confusion

How quickly can you unscramble the names of each of these countries? Each country name is a single word, so ignore any spaces in the anagrams.

**PURE**

**TANGO**

**SAILER**

**REGALIA**

**OR YAWN**

**ROAD CUE**

**POLAR GUT**

**TANGARINE**

**O ROMANCE**

**LIZARD NEWTS**

## Your architect (continued)

As you can see, executive functions form the bedrock of deliberate, complex conscious functions and are ubiquitous in their application across domains of human cognition. They are therefore regarded by some neuroscientists as the pinnacle of our cognitive evolution and key to intelligence.

When tackling tasks that are complex and new to you, it is up to your architect to learn the inner workings of how to best complete an exercise. As you become more proficient and accustomed to the approach a puzzle requires, your processing speed will increase. Whether you complete the sudoku in **'1.3: Sudoku 6×6' on page 36**, find your way to PARIS in **'1.5: Travel network' on page 38**, find complex patterns in **'1.6: Odd one out' on page 39**, or think creatively with **'1.17: What's in the box?' on page 57**, executive functions have got you covered.

# 1.3: Sudoku 6×6

Complete each of these sudoku puzzles by placing a digit from 1 to 6 into each empty square, so that no digit repeats in any row, column or bold-lined 3×2 box.

| | 3 | | | | 5 |
|---|---|---|---|---|---|
| 2 | | | | | |
| | | 6 | | 2 | |
| | 4 | | 5 | | |
| | | | | | 2 |
| 4 | | | | 6 | |

| | | | 6 | | 1 |
|---|---|---|---|---|---|
| | | | 5 | | |
| 4 | | | | 6 | |
| | 1 | | | | 4 |
| | | 2 | | | |
| 5 | | 3 | | | |

## 1.4: Dominoes

Draw along the dashed lines to divide each grid into a complete set of dominoes, from 0-0 up to 4-4. Each domino will appear exactly once, so use the cross-off charts to keep track of which dominoes have been placed.

| 2 | 0 | 4 | 4 | 0 | 4 |
|---|---|---|---|---|---|
| 3 | 2 | 1 | 3 | 0 | 2 |
| 2 | 4 | 1 | 3 | 2 | 2 |
| 0 | 0 | 3 | 1 | 4 | 0 |
| 3 | 1 | 4 | 1 | 1 | 3 |

| 3 | 3 | 2 | 4 | 2 | 2 |
|---|---|---|---|---|---|
| 3 | 3 | 1 | 4 | 0 | 0 |
| 1 | 1 | 2 | 4 | 1 | 4 |
| 1 | 3 | 0 | 0 | 1 | 4 |
| 0 | 4 | 2 | 3 | 2 | 0 |

# 1.5: Travel network

You're having trouble finding your way to Paris. Can *you* find 'PARIS' in this network? Start on any circle and then follow lines to touching circles, so that each circle visited in turn spells out the name. No circle can be revisited.

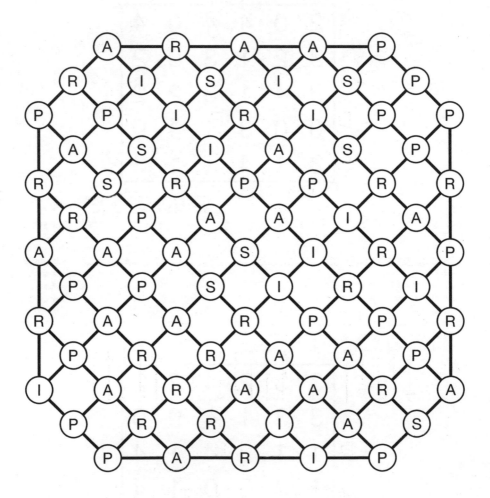

# 1.6: Odd one out

Which of the images, A to E, is the odd one out from each set
– and why?

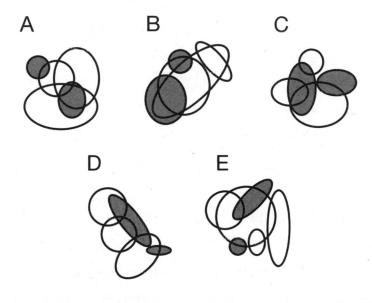

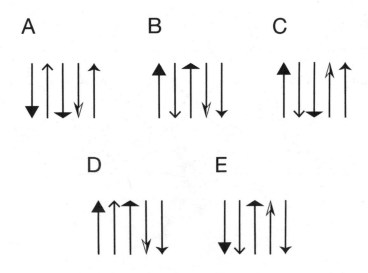

## Your sketch pad – visuospatial cognition

To find our way through our environment the brain needs to represent the spatial relationships between objects and people to prevent us from bumping into them, reaching into empty space when we try to grab that apple on the table or getting lost on our way around the grocery store. Visuospatial cognition refers to the processes that help us tackle these challenges.

Including three-dimensional puzzles in a two-dimensional book is quite the challenge. Yet, a few functions of visuospatial cognition can be practised on the page, such as mental rotation. Mental rotation and reflection tasks such as those in **'1.7: Reflect on this' on page 41** require you to manipulate visuospatial information in your 'mind's eye' to form an internal three-dimensional image of a complex object or environment. If you have read the previous section, you can already guess that these visuospatial functions are intricately linked with working memory abilities.

# 1.7: Reflect on this

Imagine reflecting each of these two images in the dashed lines shown. Which lower image, A to D, then results in each case? Ignore the changes in scale.

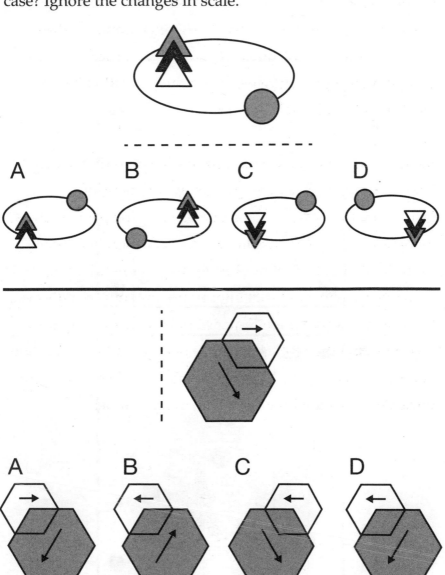

## 1.8: Shape link

In each of the two puzzles below, draw a series of separate paths that each connects a pair of identical shapes. No more than one path can enter any square, and paths can only travel horizontally or vertically between squares.

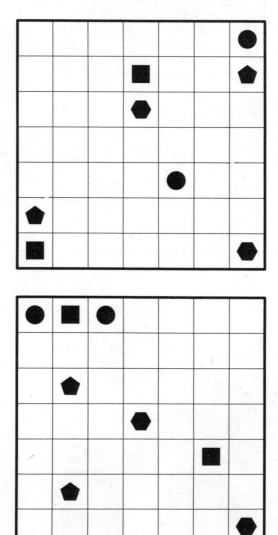

# 1.9: Top-down problem

Which of the options, A to D, represents the view of each 3D object when seen from the direction of the arrow?

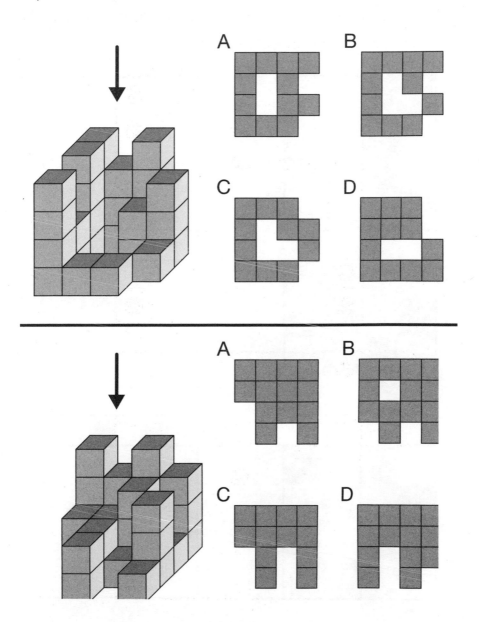

## 1.10: Grid memory

Look at the pattern in the first grid on the left of the page, then cover it over and see if you can accurately reproduce it in the empty grid to its right. Repeat similarly for the second and third grids.

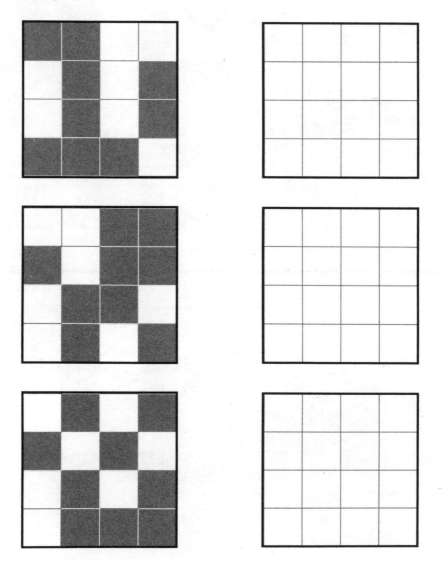

# 1.11: Building blocks

In each of the puzzles below, which set of blocks – A to D – can be rearranged to form the assembly shown? All blocks must be used exactly once each.

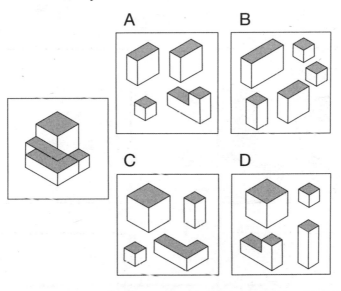

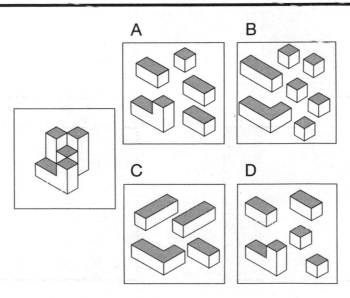

## 1.12: Fold and punch

Imagine folding and then punching paper as shown in each of the two puzzles. Unfold, and which image, A to D, results?

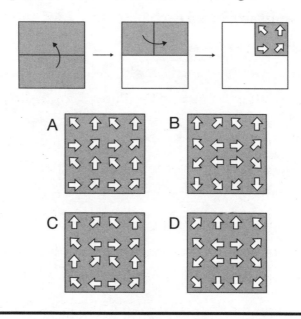

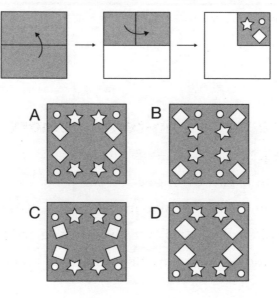

## Your sketch pad (continued)

Becoming better at forming and manipulating mental images can also help with a variety of other functions, such as using certain memory strategies to recall information more easily.

Interestingly, even learning complex science concepts is often facilitated by better visuospatial abilities. For instance:

▶ for a chemist, being able to imagine the arrangement of different elements in a molecule will benefit remembering how different substances may react with one another;

▶ in engineering, imagining how different pieces can be assembled to form a new design is crucial;

▶ and a surgeon requires an excellent mental 3D model of their patient's anatomy to make the right cut and avoid disaster.

## Your librarian – long-term memory

Learning requires storing information for the long-haul. The more you know, the more you can draw on existing knowledge and use it to solve problems, for instance by combining different pieces of information to arrive at novel conclusions and solutions. Long-term memory has

a remarkable capacity: language, facts, motor skills, your personally experienced 'autobiographical' memories, they're all stored within those billions and billions of cells.

Yet, most of what we experience every day never makes it into our permanent library. Why do we forget so much? Researchers have argued that our memory systems did not evolve to take snapshots of our world or keep a detailed journal. Doing so would take up a lot of resources and our survival simply did not depend on that. What it did depend on was:

▶ the learning of new motor skills (*Throw that spear!*);

▶ accurate and extremely fast categorization of objects, contexts and living beings (*Is that a tiger? Can I eat that berry?*);

▶ recall of inter-group relationships (*Can I trust that group member or will they try to steal my food? Who in this group gets along well; who doesn't?*);

▶ successful communication (*I run ahead and you two go left and right to cut off our prey's escape routes!*);

▶ and the use of all of this knowledge to plan ahead (*I shouldn't take those two on a hunting party because they don't work well together, so I'll take the one who is the better spear thrower*).

If you look at it from that perspective, your long-term memory does an excellent job. Nevertheless, it does get extremely frustrating having to ask a person for their name once again or having to search for your password because you don't recall it by heart. In the following chapters, you will be introduced to some helpful mnemonic strategies. For now, you can get warmed up with **'1.13: Password posers' on page 50.**

## 1.13: Password posers

Start by covering up the questions below the dividing line, then spend up to a minute memorizing these four codes and passwords. Once time is up, reveal the questions beneath.

| | |
|---|---|
| **Bank card PIN:** | **3971** |
| **Email password:** | **D14MoND** |
| **Alarm passcode:** | **468123** |
| **Work password:** | **o1f2f3i4c5e** |

## Recall

Cover over the top part of the page. Then, see if you can answer the following questions:

1. **What was the bank card PIN?**
2. **What word does the email password spell out, swapping digits for similar-looking letters?**
3. **What six-letter word is contained within the 'Work' password, alternating with the digits?**
4. **Which digit appears in all four of the passwords?**
5. **If you added together the six digits in the alarm passcode, what would the total be?**
6. **Which code/password contained only odd digits?**

# 1.14: F is for (not) forgetting

Start by covering everything beneath the dividing line on this page. Then, study this list of animals until you think you have memorized it completely. Once you're ready, cover up the list and reveal the instructions below the divider.

**Fox**
**Frog**
**Fossa**
**Ferret**
**Firefly**
**Flamingo**

# Recall

Now can you rewrite the list you have just memorized, writing out the animals in the same order? The underlines show you how many letters there are in each name.

# 1.15: Grimm recall

Before you begin, cover the text on the opposite page. Now read the following text, abridged from *Grimms' Fairy Tales*, a few times until you think you will remember the phrasing used. Then, continue opposite.

'A king and queen once upon a time reigned in a country where there were in those days fairies. Now this king and queen had plenty of money, and plenty of fine clothes to wear, and plenty of good things to eat and drink: but though they had been married many years they had no children, and this grieved them very much indeed.

One day, as the queen was walking by the side of the river, she saw a poor little fish that had thrown itself out of the water, and lay gasping and nearly dead on the bank. The queen took pity on the little fish, and threw it back again into the river; and before it swam away it lifted its head out of the water and said, "I know what your wish is, and it shall be fulfilled, in return for your kindness to me – you will soon have a daughter." What the little fish had foretold soon came to pass; and the queen had a little girl, so very beautiful that the king could not cease looking on it for joy.'

## Recall

Now cover the opposite page. The text below is almost identical to the original you have just memorized, except that ten of the words in the passage have been changed. Which ten words, and can you remember what they were before?

'A king and queen once upon a time reigned in a citadel where there were in those days pixies. Now this king and queen had plenty of money, and plenty of ridiculous clothes to wear, and plenty of good things to eat and drink: but though they had been married twenty years they had no children, and this annoyed them very much indeed.

One day, as the queen was walking by the side of the river, she saw a poor little fish that had thrown itself out of the water, and lay giggling and nearly dead on the bank. The queen took pity on the hilarious fish, and threw it back again into the waterfall; and before it swam away it lifted its head out of the water and said, "I know what your wish is, and it shall be fulfilled, in return for your kindness to me – you will soon have a son." What the little fish had foretold soon came to pass; and the queen had a little boy, so very beautiful that the king could not cease looking on it for joy.'

## 1.16: Grocery genius

Start by covering everything beneath the dividing line on this page. Then, study this list of groceries until you think you have memorized it completely. Once you're ready, cover up the list and reveal the instructions below the divider.

| | |
|---|---|
| **Apples** | **Eggs** |
| **Bananas** | **Flatbread** |
| **Carrots** | **Grapes** |
| **Donuts** | **Halloumi** |

## Recall

Now, can you rewrite the list you have just memorized, writing out the items in the same order? The first letter of each item has been given to help you.

**A**........................................

**B**........................................

**C**........................................

**D**........................................

**E**........................................

**F**........................................

**G**........................................

**H**........................................

## Your out-of-the-box thinker – creative problem solving

Around three million years ago, *homo habilis* was the first known species of our close ancestors that came up with unusual uses for the common objects in the environment and fashioned them into tools. This was a huge feat of creative thinking: the ability to imagine a desired outcome and novel solutions.

Of course, human creativity does not only produce practical solutions to the problems we face; it also generates works of art merely because we find them aesthetically pleasing. Almost any culture we know has their own works of art, suggesting that creativity may be an inherent property of our brain. Being creative provided us with an edge over the competition as humans faced a variety of complex challenges in their struggle to survive.

Increasing your creativity to produce beautiful, aesthetic works of art is a worthwhile goal in its own right but it has less to do with puzzles. This book focuses on exercises that are known to promote creative thinking in a way that it allows for new approaches to problems. This process is also termed 'lateral thinking'. It is separate from traditional logical thinking and reasoning because it may not be

obtained from a step-by-step approach using all the available evidence within a given problem. Essentially, creativity allows out-of-the-box thinking.

Here, you can begin warming up and getting your creative juices going by thinking about **'1.17: What's in the box?' on page 57** and then get to what's outside it in **'1.18: Object-ive thinking' on page 58.**

# 1.17: What's in the box?

Draw in the boxes to show what you think is inside them.

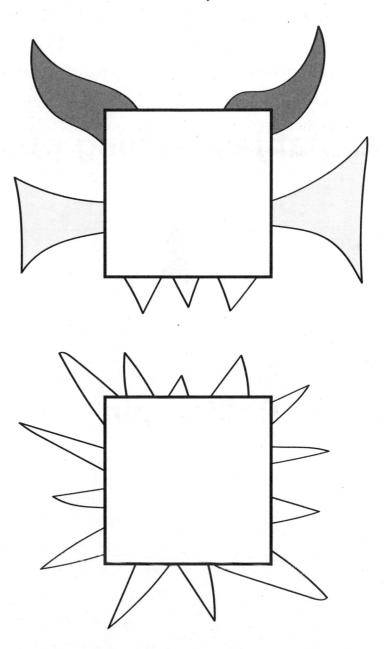

## 1.18: Object-ive thinking

How many unusual uses can you think of for each of the objects listed below? Write down as many as you can think of, and try to avoid including anything that the object in question would 'normally' be used for.

# Inflatable paddling pool

..................................................................................................................

..................................................................................................................

..................................................................................................................

..................................................................................................................

# Rolling pin

..................................................................................................................

..................................................................................................................

..................................................................................................................

..................................................................................................................

# Your logician – reasoning skills

Reasoning involves using information to arrive at logical conclusions. Using logical thinking we can discover regularities in the world around us which can be used to make predictions about what will happen in the future and to carefully plan ways in which we can achieve our goals. Scientists who study the evolution of early humans and our biological ancestors have suggested that living in social groups, in which coordinated action was key to our survival, was an important factor in developing our reasoning skills. So, what constitutes logical reasoning? There are different types of logical reasoning. For instance, you may be given a rule that you know to be true and which you then apply to solve a given problem. Take sudoku: the rule is clearly defined and all you have to do is follow it to successfully arrive at a solution to the problem – see **'1.3: Sudoku 6×6' on page 36**. Common problems of arithmetic require these types of reasoning skills, although sudoku itself does not involve any pure mathematical deductions – the digits in it act purely as symbols.

# 1.19: Number pyramid

Write a number in each empty block, so that every block (above the bottom level) is equal to the sum of the two blocks directly beneath it.

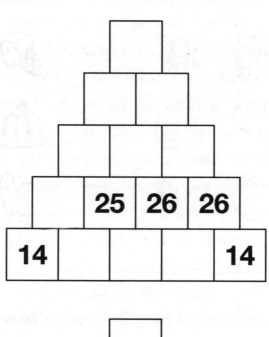

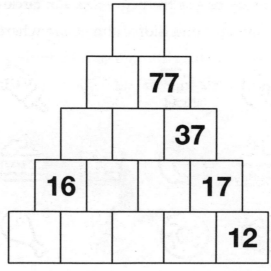

# 1.20: Food swap

Cover the bottom half of this page, then spend a minute or two studying this set of food-related images. Once you're ready, cover them up and read below.

# Recall

Now cover the top half of the page. Can you circle the images below which are new, and didn't appear anywhere above?

## Your logician (continued)

What is much more challenging is to use information we acquire about the world to further our understanding of the rules that govern it. For instance, in puzzle **'1.6: Odd one out' on page 39** you observe the evidence given to you and from it must derive a rule that describes the organization of the shapes in four out of the five arrangements. This requires much more cognitive effort than a sudoku because there is more uncertainty about what constitutes 'truth'.

## Let's take a breather

That was a lot of information dumped on you. It's basically a crash course in some of the core modules you would take if you decided to enrol in cognitive psychology and neuroscience classes. Well done for getting through them! But reading is one thing, remembering another. Coming back to this information after having worked through more pages of the book will help refresh your memory. In the next sections, you will be introduced to strategies that can help you get through these puzzles more effectively.

# 1.21: What's missing?

The eight boxes below contain eight steps in a logical sequence which has been jumbled out of order. One of the boxes is empty, however. Draw the correct picture in it.

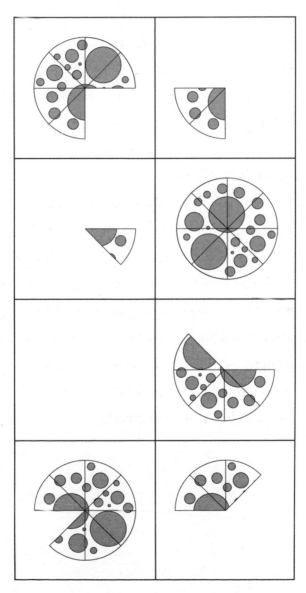

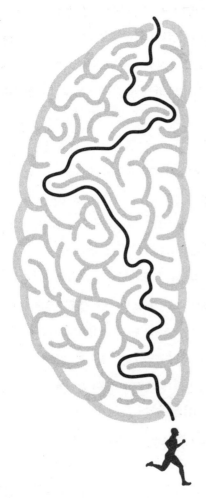

# 2.

# GETTING
# GOING

## *Getting going*

Now that your warm-up is complete, let's ramp up the difficulty. This is where you get to properly flex your cognitive muscle. You will also be introduced to the first cognitive strategies you can try on these tasks.

## Measure your progress

As you progress through these exercises and the next chapter, you may want to measure your progress. You can use the section at the back of the book, **'Your progress notes' on page 188**, to keep notes if you wish. One way of doing so may be timing yourself to see how long it takes you to complete similar tasks. Do you see a difference between your first day and a week later? How about two weeks or longer? Or do you find yourself generating more novel ideas in the creative thinking tasks? Recall more details from a previous memory task? Nothing is more motivating than seeing how far you have come, so make sure to celebrate your success when you notice you have made progress, even if it's just small steps.

## Keep holding on

The limited capacity of our short-term memory buffer that keeps information 'online' as to allow you to navigate through daily life acts as a filter which keeps you from

getting overwhelmed by the myriad of stimuli around you. When you are listening to your favourite song while waiting for the bus, you don't also need to keep in mind the faces of the strangers around you, their conversations, or the smells coming from a nearby bakery.

Yet, the vulnerability of our short-term memory systems also has the major drawback that we often need to focus if we don't want to forget what we just experienced. Focus is of course afforded by attention, a universal resource needed for all your complex cognitive functions. Unfortunately, the book format does not lend itself to attention training well, so the best you can do now to free up your resources is to minimize distractions and avoid switching between your cognitive exercises and other tasks or actions.

The most obvious strategy to use in short-term memory tasks is 'sub-vocal rehearsal'. It boils down to repeating the information over and over in your head to make sure it sticks. You probably use that one all the time. Another prominent and effective strategy for short-term memory is chunking, by which multiple elements are grouped into one chunk. Why is this effective? Bound pieces of information take up fewer resources of your short-term memory store. The simplest example is remembering the sequence 4-3-6-1

with four elements vs. remembering 43 and 61 separately as two elements. Try the following puzzle using the chunking technique.

## 2.1: Digital Memorization

Read through each of these numbers twice, chunking any memorable groups of two or more digits as you go. Then, cover this page and rewrite the digits as accurately as you can on the opposite page. Once done, repeat with each set on this page in turn.

**Test 1**

# 3 1 5 7 9 1 9 4 5

**Test 2**

# 2 0 9 9 4 2 4 5 1 8

**Test 2**

# 1 7 4 5 5 9 2 4 0 9 3

**Test 4**

# 5 2 8 5 2 0 2 5 7 8 3 9

# *Digital Recall*

Now recall the digit sequences as well as you can:

**Test 1**

........................................................................................................................................................

**Test 2**

........................................................................................................................................................

**Test 3**

........................................................................................................................................................

**Test 4**

........................................................................................................................................................

# In your mind's eye

Classic examples of visuospatial skills involve the popular 1980s game Tetris, similar types of block puzzles, or the Rubik's Cube. In contrast to verbal short-term memory, visuospatial tasks have the added complexity of requiring recall of both the identity of individual elements and the relationships between them. The chunking strategy also works for some types of visuospatial tasks. You can try it over the next few puzzles and see whether this approach works for you. For some puzzles such as Grid memory this will work well: for instance, the symmetry along the diagonal of the grid in the middle provides an easy opportunity for chunking. Your brain has a preference for familiar grouping of shapes, so diagonals, Ts, rectangles and triangles are easily chunked together. Even more memorable are shapes that are reminiscent of meaningful objects.

Not all strategies are equally effective for a given cognitive task, as you will see in the following puzzles. Learning how to select the most appropriate strategy is in itself a worthwhile goal and something you can strive for as you work your way through these puzzles.

# 2.2: Grid memory

Look at the pattern in the first grid on the left of the page, then cover it over and see if you can accurately reproduce it in the empty grid to its right. Repeat similarly for the second and third grids.

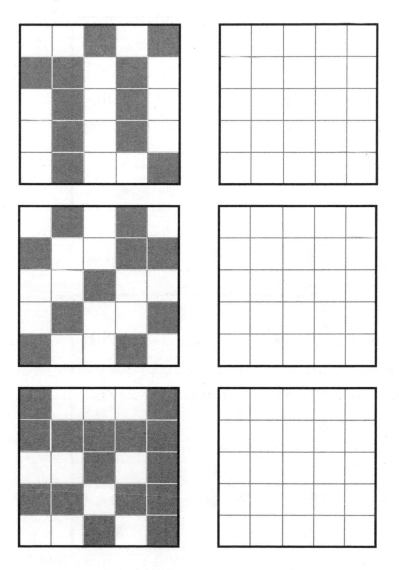

POINTS

## 2.3: Shape link

In each of the two puzzles below, draw a series of separate paths that each connects a pair of identical shapes. No more than one path can enter any square, and paths can only travel horizontally or vertically between squares.

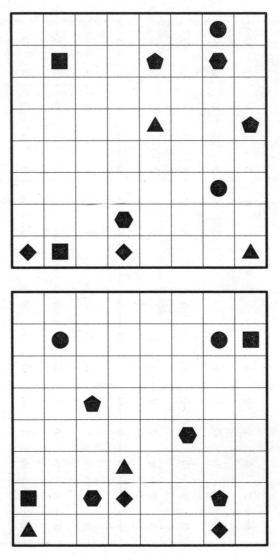

## 2.4: Fences

Draw horizontal and vertical lines to join all of the dots in each grid into a single loop which visits every dot exactly once, and does not cross itself. Some lines are already given.

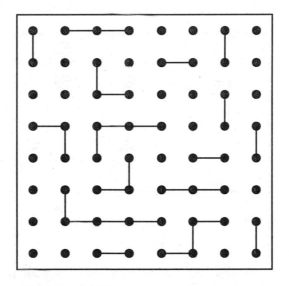

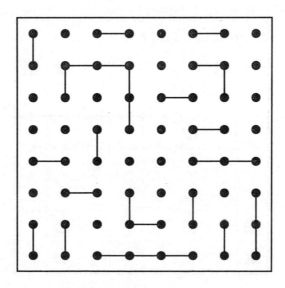

# Transformative

Other classic tasks to train your visuospatial skills involve mental rotation: picturing a stimulus in your mind's eye and manipulating it to change its orientation. In **'2.5: Hidden image' on page** 75, the shape and configuration of the hidden objects remain constant. Rather, the goal is to rotate them to test whether they in fact appear in one of the four options. To do so, you can employ an analytical strategy in which you separately process each part of the shape and rotate it on its own to match up against parts of another exemplar. Or aim for a holistic strategy in which you rotate the shape as a whole. However, this may become more challenging with larger shapes.

For those who loathe spatial tasks, describing individual steps verbally may work better because it transforms the material into an additional representation that can be maintained separately from the visual information. Using your hands to mimic the moves you would need for the different parts of the shape (a 'kinesthetic' strategy) uses yet another processing system to come to your aid.

## 2.5: Hidden image

Which of the options, A to D, conceals the image shown on the far left of each puzzle? It may be rotated but all elements of it must be visible.

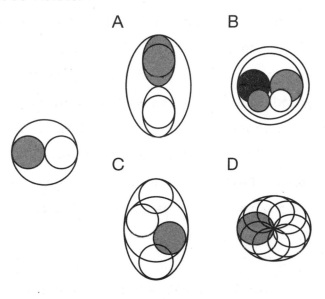

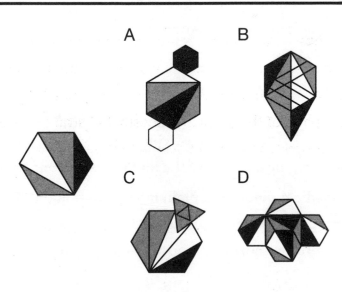

## Transformative (continued)

In visuospatial construction tasks, your goal is to change the configuration of objects to create something new: a cube or some other shape, such as in **'1.11: Building blocks' on page 45 in the previous chapter**, or in folding over the surface in **'2.6: Tracing paper' on page 77**. These are fundamental skills for anyone working with 3D objects and are essentially a more abstract form of building with Lego or putting together an IKEA shelf.

## Multiple memory systems

Throughout our lives we amass quite the sizeable collection of long-term memories which are organized in different subsystems of the brain.

▶ **Procedural memory** – such as writing, riding a bicycle, knitting, playing tennis or the piano – supports your motor skills.

▶ **Semantic memory** is your archive for facts and knowledge and by virtue of partially overlapping brain networks it works in close collaboration with episodic memory, the steward of the memories of your past.

▶ **Episodic memories** contain information about the context of a specific episode and the details therein, while semantic memories are mostly detached from the context

## 2.6: Tracing paper

Which of the options, A to D, represents the view of each image shown to the left when folded in half along the dashed line? Assume it has been drawn on transparent paper.

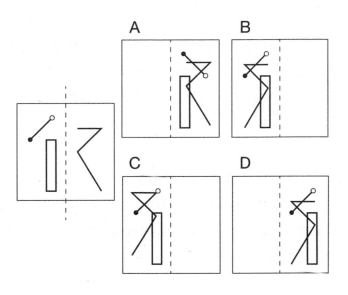

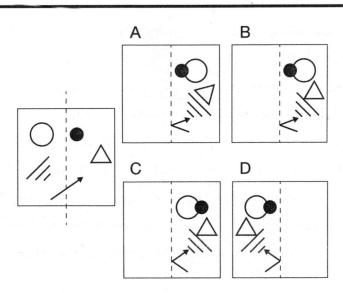

in which we first learned them. While the Shakespearean shakedown requires only memory for facts, Sherlock's *A Study in Scarlet* demands recall of context and details of the narrative.

Other neural systems and cognitive processes work hand in hand with long-term memory. For instance, unscrambling anagrams does not only test your ability to quickly rifle through your factual knowledge, it also demands you keep subsequent candidates in mind and simultaneously use your visuospatial working memory to swap around letters to test whether your guess is correct. Not only does this tax your short- and long-term memory abilities, if you add the timing element to it, these types of puzzles also train the speed with which your brain processes information.

## 2.7: Musical medleys

How quickly can you unscramble the names of these famous musicians? The word lengths of each unscrambled name are given in brackets after the anagram.

# AND MOAN (7)

# LIVELY SPREES (5, 7)

# EVEN WORDIEST (6, 6)

# NO HEN JOLT (5, 4)

# SEEN HEARD (2, 7)

# ARTY IT FLOWS (6, 5)

# PARTY ON DOLL (5, 6)

# CURT MANLY PACE (4, 9)

## 2.8: A study in scarlet

Before you begin, cover the text on the opposite page. Now read the following text, taken from *A Study in Scarlet* by Arthur Conan Doyle, a few times until you think you will remember the phrasing used. Then, continue opposite.

'Holmes was certainly not a difficult man to live with. He was quiet in his ways, and his habits were regular. It was rare for him to be up after ten at night, and he had invariably breakfasted and gone out before I rose in the morning.

Sometimes he spent his day at the chemical laboratory, sometimes in the dissecting-rooms, and occasionally in long walks, which appeared to take him into the lowest portions of the City.

Nothing could exceed his energy when the working fit was upon him; but now and again a reaction would seize him, and for days on end he would lie upon the sofa in the sitting room, hardly uttering a word or moving a muscle from morning to night. On these occasions I have noticed such a dreamy, vacant expression in his eyes, that I might have suspected him of being addicted to the use of some narcotic, had not the temperance and cleanliness of his whole life forbidden such a notion.'

## *Recall*

Now cover the opposite page. The text below is almost identical to the original you have just memorized, except that eight of the words in the passage have been changed. Which eight words, and can you say what they were before?

'Holmes was certainly not a hard man to live with. He was quiet in his ways, and his habits were predictable. It was rare for him to be up after ten at night, and he had invariably eaten and gone out before I rose in the morning.

Sometimes he spent his day at the biology laboratory, sometimes in the dissecting-rooms, and occasionally in long walks, which appeared to take him into the lowest portions of the town.

Nothing could exceed his energy when the working fit was upon him; but now and again a reaction would grab him, and for days on end he would lie upon the sofa in the living room, hardly uttering a word or moving a muscle from morning to night. On these occasions I have noticed such a dreamy, empty expression in his eyes, that I might have suspected him of being addicted to the use of some narcotic, had not the temperance and cleanliness of his whole life forbidden such a notion.'

## 2.9: Shakespearean shakedown

Which eight plays by William Shakespeare have been clued below, where only the first letter of each word in a play's title has been given?

AYLI

MAAN

AMND

TTNK

TTOTS

TTGOV

AWTEW

TMWOW

## Bonded for life

Sometimes we may find ourselves wander among the halls
of our archive and without any external impulse retrieve
a record from our episodic memory while we reminisce.
In most instances though, we recall episodic memories
because we are prompted by a cue that activates a trace of the
memory representation stored in our mental library.

We may have seen, heard, smelled or tasted something that
reminds us of a past event. If this sensation has a strong
association with that experience, it can trigger a particularly
vivid memory:

▶ Maybe you often ate a particular flavour of ice cream
   during a summer holiday;

▶ Maybe you and your best friend have that one song that
   is 'your song', that makes you think of the good times
   you shared;

▶ Maybe a famous quote from a movie reminds you of the
   first time you ever saw that film in the cinema ('May the
   Force be with you!'; 'I'll be back!'; 'Shaken, not stirred.').

These types of cues are like laser pointers to a particular
memory or multiple related memories in your archive
and they often simultaneously bring back a host of details

associated with that memory. You can even use that memory
to more easily jump to recalling similar instances, starting
a chain reaction of memory dominoes. This will be an
enormous advantage over attempting to recall a memory
without a strong cue, for which you have to engage in a
much more exhaustive search of the contents of your archive.
This is why **'2.10: 'C' how your memory is' on page 86**
is much simpler than **'2.11: Fifteen words and minutes' on
page 87**: the starting letter C limits your memory search
space.

The best ways to form powerful memory cues is to create
associations between pieces of information you hope to
recall. Combining this strategy with vivid mental imagery is
even more effective.

Think of ways in which you can form associations between
the images and words in **'2.12: Food swap' on page 88** or
the words in the list in **'2.11: Fifteen words and minutes'
on page 87**. Can they be combined by an action (throwing
the suitcase out the window)? Do they share commonalities
(a sticker and a ruler can be found in an office)? Can you
connect them in a story with both words and pictures in your
head?

This method is particularly effective if the narrative is odd or funny ('When he woke up in the morning to weigh himself, he stepped on a banana that was placed on the scale' ).

Can they be associated with an existing memory of yours (on my last train journey, I spilled coffee over my seat)? Forming associations, elaborating on the to-be-remembered information and building narratives can help us recall more information in a more holistic and long-lasting manner.

# 2.10: 'C' how your memory is

Start by covering everything beneath the dividing line on this page. Then, study this list of words until you think you have memorized it completely. Once you're ready, cover up the list and reveal the instructions below the divider.

| | |
|---|---|
| **Cerulean** | **Coconut** |
| **Cabbage** | **Crockery** |
| **Creative** | **Continent** |
| **Crumble** | **Cypress** |

# Recall

Now can you rewrite the list you have just memorized, but now writing out the same items in alphabetical order? The first two letters of each item have been given to help you.

**Ca**......................................

**Ce**......................................

**Co**......................................

**Co**......................................

**Cr**......................................

**Cr**......................................

**Cr**......................................

**Cy**......................................

## 2.11: Fifteen words and minutes

Start by taking as long as you need to memorize the following 15 words, then carry on reading below.

| | |
|:---:|:---:|
| **Imagination** | **Elbow** |
| **Sticker** | **Stick** |
| **Process** | **Category** |
| **Ruler** | **Television** |
| **Keyboard** | **Hat** |
| **Radiation** | **Plenty** |
| **Crossing** | **Storage** |

**Love**

## Recall

Now cover up the above, and try to recall all 15 words:

........................................   ........................................

........................................   ........................................

........................................   ........................................

........................................   ........................................

........................................   ........................................

........................................   ........................................

........................................   ........................................

........................................

## And then

Wait 15 minutes, and turn to page 105.

## 2.12: Food swap

Cover the bottom half of this page, then spend some time studying these images and the word associated with each image. Once you're ready, cover them up and read below.

Marigold     Pencil     Banana

Shirt     Truck     Leaf

Window     Tennis     Coffee

## Recall

Now cover the top half of the page. Can you fill the gap below each image with the same word that was used above?

## 2.13: State swap

Start by covering everything beneath the dividing line on this page. Then, study this list of countries until you think you have memorized it completely. Once you're ready, cover up the list and reveal the instructions below the divider.

| | |
|---|---|
| **Indonesia** | **Brazil** |
| **Argentina** | **Malawi** |
| **Hungary** | **Jordan** |
| **Japan** | **Mexico** |
| **Norway** | **Oman** |
| **Canada** | **New Zealand** |
| **Sierra Leone** | **Portugal** |

## Recall

Here is the same list, but now some of the countries have been replaced with others – and the list is in a different order. Can you circle the new countries? As a bonus, can you also say which countries they replaced?

| | |
|---|---|
| **Argentina** | **Malawi** |
| **Brazil** | **Montenegro** |
| **Canada** | **Norway** |
| **Hungary** | **Oman** |
| **India** | **Papa New Guinea** |
| **Japan** | **Portugal** |
| **Jordan** | **Sierra Leone** |

## 2.14: Password posers

Start by covering up the opposite page, then attempt to memorize as many of codes and passwords as you can. Once you feel ready, cover over this page and reveal the page opposite instead.

**Phone unlock PIN: 038562**

**Online banking password: rebmemeR1001**

**WiFi password: 10int29er38net47pass56**

**Laptop login code: l3tm31n**

**TV streaming PIN: m4o5v6i7e**

**Work email password: topsecret1995**

**Utility bills PIN: 000884**

**Home computer password: Home72Screen**

## *Recall*

The same codes and passwords are shown again below, but each of them has been modified in some way. Can you spot the change to each line and say what the original code or password was? The list is given in the same order.

**Phone unlock PIN: 039562**

**Online banking password: RebmemeR1001**

**WiFi password: 10int29ern38et47pass56**

**Laptop login code: l3tM31n**

**TV streaming PIN: m4o5v6i7e8**

**Work email password: topsecret1999**

**Utility bills PIN: 008884**

**Home computer password: Homes72Screen**

## The critical thinker

Logic and reasoning allow you to put two and two together to arrive at correct conclusions about the world. Finding these rules and patterns in the information around us is key to making predictions and solving complex problems. You can think of the brain as a superb prediction machine which constantly accumulates new data to check whether its knowledge about the world is up to date and which uses these predictions to guide your behaviour. Making a prediction ahead of time allows you to act more quickly to events in your environment and to plan accordingly. For instance, if you know that the next train will leave in ten minutes, but you need twelve minutes to walk to the station, you can conclude that you will not be able to make it in time to catch your train by walking. But maybe you can jump on your bicycle instead.

Let's start with some numeric logic problems.

POINTS

## 2.15: *Sudoku*

Complete this sudoku puzzle by placing a digit from 1 to 9 into each empty square, so that no digit repeats in any row, column or bold-lined 3×3 box.

| 4 | 1 |   |   | 6 |   |   | 9 | 5 |
|---|---|---|---|---|---|---|---|---|
| 9 |   | 5 |   |   |   | 6 |   | 4 |
|   | 3 |   |   |   |   |   | 2 |   |
|   |   |   | 8 |   | 9 |   |   |   |
| 8 |   |   |   |   |   |   |   | 3 |
|   |   |   | 6 |   | 5 |   |   |   |
|   | 2 |   |   |   |   |   | 1 |   |
| 1 |   | 4 |   |   |   | 8 |   | 2 |
| 3 | 8 |   |   | 5 |   |   | 4 | 9 |

# 2.16: Number pyramid

Write a number in each empty block, so that every block (above the bottom level) is equal to the sum of the two blocks directly beneath it.

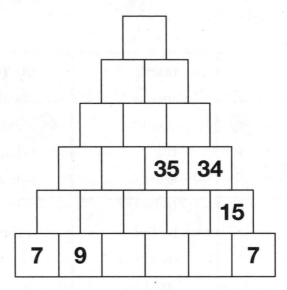

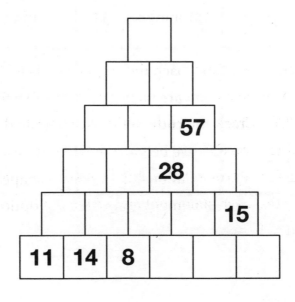

# The critical thinker (continued)

In contrast to sudoku, the following visuospatial abstract reasoning puzzles do not give you a rule. You have to crack the code on your own. Tasks like these are often used in intelligence (IQ) tests.

Although there is not just one type of intelligence (consider linguistic or social intelligence for instance), tests of reasoning that involve these types of visuospatial material have the advantage that they do not rely on language and are less influenced by cultural differences between people around the world. They also tend to be those indicators most tightly linked to performance in the fields of science, technology, engineering and maths. However, the people who excel at these types of logical tests are not necessarily the same ones who stand out when reasoning tasks involve language.

The simplest way to approach these exercises is to write down the steps you are using to try to solve them. Consider '2.17: Crack the code' on page 97: write down commonalities you observe between images, note all options that may describe true relationships between shapes and letters, then test each statement and strike out options you have found to be wrong.

Be careful to also look for evidence that could disprove your idea about the rule. Once they have a suspicion, most people only search for evidence in favour but not against their hypothesis, which is a common fallacy called *confirmation bias* that permeates much of our reasoning in everyday life.

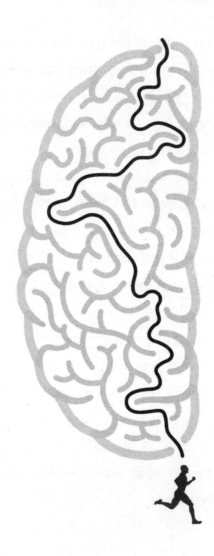

## 2.17: Crack the code

Crack the code used to describe each image, and pick which option, 'a' to 'd', should replace the question mark.

ZQK

FRK

FQP

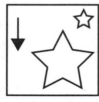

ZMK

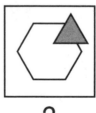

?

a. FQK   b. ZMP

c. ZRP   d. FRK

WLX

RQH

WLH

RLX

?

a. WLH   b. RQX

c. RLQ   d. WQX

# 2.18: Complete the sequence

Which of the options, A to E, should be placed in the empty box on each top row in order to create a logical sequence?

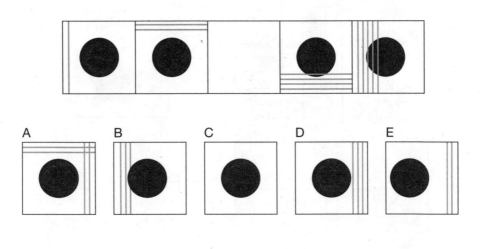

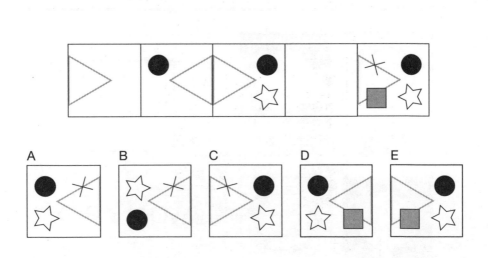

## 2.19: Complete the square

Which of the four options, A to D, should be placed into the empty square in each grid to complete the pattern?

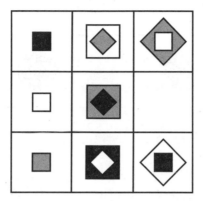

A   B   C   D

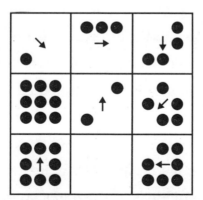

A   B 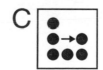  C   D

## Your inner child to the rescue

The mind of a child is truly amazing in its creative potential.
When we were children, mundane objects could become tools
that were entirely removed from their original purpose. We
would conjure up new worlds, give voices to our puppets
and plush animals, dress up as warriors to save the world.
Who cares if we ran around squealing, wearing a metal
strainer on our head to protect it from the attack of a dragon?
But we all have to grow up at some point and use that
wooden spoon for stirring sizzling food in a pan rather than
waving it in the air to work a magic spell.

Famous creativity researcher Robert McKim at Stanford
University ran an experiment in which he asked university
students to draw the person sitting next to them in class.
He called 'stop' after thirty seconds, leading to much
embarrassed laughter and calls of 'I'm sorry!'. Clearly, the
adults in the room were worried about what others thought
of their creation. Would this have happened with children?
The answer is a resounding no.

That fear of being judged, especially when we come up with
unusual thoughts and ideas, is the foe of creativity. We don't
take as many risks anymore and as a result lose freedom
in our thinking. This is even the case when you create

something only for yourself alone, knowing that no one else will ever get to see it. Most likely, you have internalized this judgemental attitude towards your ideas. On the one hand, it makes sense that we don't just blurt out the first thing that comes to mind. On the other hand, if we censor ourselves too much then we stop offering novel ideas. It may just seem too risky. Design firms have realized this as a major problem, and many are now fostering a more relaxed, friendly, less judgemental environment. After all, if we feel less judged we may be less anxious to share a design or new idea with our peers – even if it seems quite wacky.

A good approach to reduce the influence of your inner critic on your ideas is to give yourself a time limit to generate as many solutions to a problem as possible. It will help you suppress your tendency to second guess yourself because your goal is to go for quantity and do so quickly. A great example of a creativity task that helps you loosen up and suppress that inner critic is **'2.21: Eighteen circles' on page 103** in which you have three minutes to transform eighteen empty circles into objects.

Another classic exercise is to come up with as many unusual uses of a common object. It's clear what the intended use of a paper clip is, but there are so many others, like using the wire

as a lock pick, removing dirt from under your fingernails (a valid response despite the unappetizing image this may elicit), opening that pesky slit in which you place your SIM card in an iPhone, and on and on it goes. If your inner critic tends to be particularly strong, you can also complete '**2.20: Object-ive thinking' below** by setting yourself a time limit.

POINTS

## 2.20: Object-ive thinking

How many unusual uses can you think of for the object listed below? Write down as many as you can think of, and try to avoid including anything that the object in question would 'normally' be used for.

# Desk lamp

..............................................................................................................

..............................................................................................................

..............................................................................................................

..............................................................................................................

..............................................................................................................

## 2.21: Eighteen circles

Using purely your creative imagination, draw as many varied pictures as you can that each use one of the circles below.

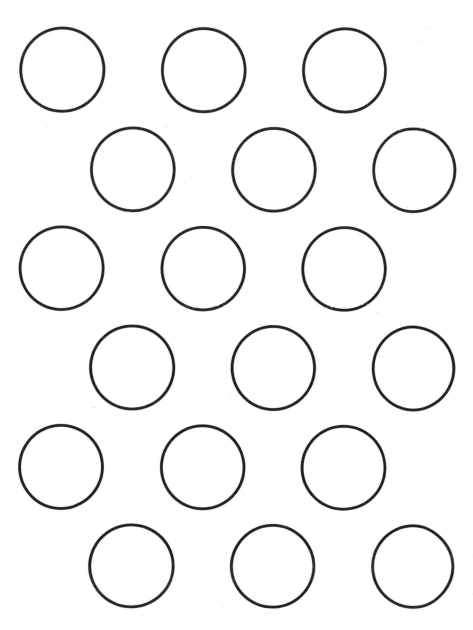

## Your inner child to the rescue (continued)

Once you completed such a task, you can reflect on your solutions. Do they share a common theme or are they variations of the same idea, such as a soccer ball, basketball, tennis ball, as responses to the Eighteen Circles exercise? Besides fluency (the speed with which you generate ideas), in subsequent exercises you should also aim for flexibility, meaning greater diversity of your ideas. If you have friends or family members who are happy to try this exercise as well, share your creations and see if you managed to come up with unique designs and uses. This will also help you overcome the fear of sharing your creative ideas.

# *Recall (continued from page 87)*

If you have not already attempted the exercise on page 87 then please complete that first.

Once 15 minutes has passed, how many of the 15 words can you still remember? Write as many as you can on the 15 lines below.

...............................................

...............................................

...............................................

...............................................

...............................................

...............................................

...............................................

...............................................

...............................................

...............................................

...............................................

...............................................

...............................................

...............................................

...............................................

# 2.22: Cube counting

How many cubes are there in each of the following images? Each began as a 4×4×4 block before some cubes were removed. None of the cubes are 'floating' in mid-air.

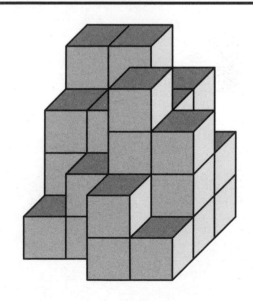

# 2.23: What's missing?

The eight boxes below contain eight steps in a logical sequence which has been jumbled out of order. One of the boxes is empty, however. Draw the correct picture in it.

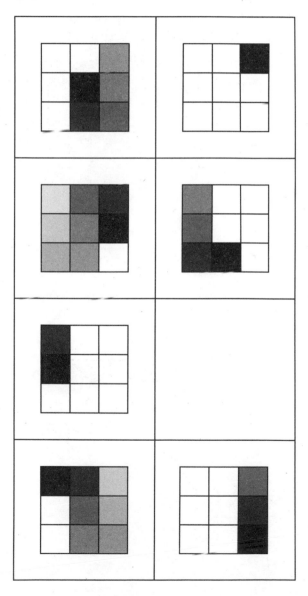

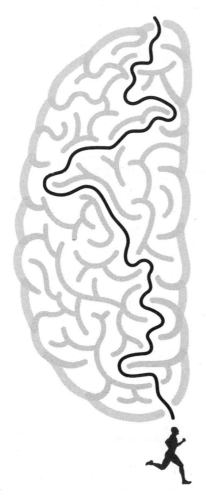

# 3.

# CARDIO

# *Cardio*

Are you ready to take on the most demanding tasks in our 'cardio' challenge? Of course, 'cardio' means heart rather than brain, but it's still a useful term to get you to picture a demanding, high-intensity exercise meant to help you make progress.

Hopefully, before you start the puzzles in this chapter, you will have completed some of the warm-up exercises and moved on to some of the more challenging puzzles in Chapter 2. Here, the goal is to challenge yourself even more, apply the strategies you already know and learn new ones. The puzzles are intended to be difficult but will hopefully become easier with time and practice.

## Dealing with adversity

When you feel overwhelmed by any of these exercises, take your time to solve the puzzle, mull it over, maybe come back to it after a break. Sometimes entering a new environment can help us to come up with new ideas. Splitting up tasks into sub-components can be helpful in isolating particular aspects of a problem and working through them step by step. Especially for reasoning tasks, rephrasing the problems in your own words, writing them down yourself and

organizing them into a structure that feels intuitive to you may be initial steps for particularly tricky exercises.

Let's jump in!

## Best buddies

Short- and long-term memory are good pals: when we recall an old memory its contents are held 'online' in a consciously accessible state by short-term memory. We can use this connection to our advantage. If you are given a list of digits such as the six numbers in the phone PIN in **'3.1: Password posers' on page 112** you can try to recall them by rehearsing them in your head and applying the chunking technique, but you can also draw on your long-term memory to create a meaningful connection between the numbers and your prior knowledge. Born in 1962? Live in number 85 in your street? Now you can draw on both the chunking method and information that is meaningful to you and that you won't forget easily. This will also make it more likely that you can remember the information in the long run. The same goes when you can find patterns that govern the information you try to recall (1-3-5-7 is much easier to remember than 9-2-6-0). Can you find any in the WiFi password? What happens if you come back to those tomorrow or next week?

## 3.1: Password posers

Return to the memory exercise on page 90 and attempt to memorize all of the codes and passwords. Once you think you have done so, return here and complete the following:

### Phone unlock PIN:

.............................................................................................

### Online banking password:

.............................................................................................

### WiFi password:

.............................................................................................

### Laptop login code:

.............................................................................................

### TV streaming PIN:

.............................................................................................

### Work email password:

.............................................................................................

### Utility bills PIN:

.............................................................................................

### Home computer password:

.............................................................................................

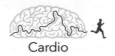
## 3.2: Olympic scramble

How quickly can you unscramble the names of these Olympic sports, which may feature at either the Summer or Winter Games? Each sport's name is a single word, so ignore any spaces in the anagrams.

# GLUE

# LION BATH

# MIND TO BAN

# CHEAT LIST

# KEEN SLOT

# I WRONG

# QUIET EARNS

# BOO WINS GRAND

# BRAKE SAINT GOD

# The art of storytelling

As you now know, different mnemonic strategies lend themselves to different types of material. To recall details and facts from text passages you may use the *PQRST* strategy. It stands for Preview, Question, Read, State and Test. This technique has originally been used to aid students' reading comprehension, but it can also help you to recall information from a text at a later time. In a rapid **Preview** of the text, you quickly identify the overarching theme which serves as a memory scaffold, drawing on your general background knowledge that is already solidly anchored in your mental library. You then formulate **Questions** about the information in the text which more actively engages you as opposed to reading in a more passive voice. It also sharpens your focus on specific elements of the text. You should then **Read** the text more carefully and **State** your answers to the questions you formulated. Finally, you can **Test** yourself on the amount of recalled information. You will see, posing questions = richer story telling.

Although making acronyms of more complex terms is a helpful memory strategy in itself, what happens when the acronym is too long and you can't even remember your memory aid? Creating something more memorable like a sentence with semantic meaning is an even more powerful

tool. You may easily forget each step for this strategy if you only have the letters *PQRST* to go on but if you instead try to remember it by the 'posing questions = richer story telling' method, you are more likely to recall each step. If you can find one, a rhyming sentence is even better – no wonder you probably recall the lyrics to countless songs!

For the following memory puzzles try out these new strategies. Use what you have learned in Chapter 2 and draw on strategies that strengthen associations, paint vivid mental images and stories, and organize material into a format that suits you best to commit it to long-term memory. For **'3.24: Face off' on page 146**, try to form associations between a name and the specific features and idiosyncrasies of the person: Dave has spikey hair like a crown. Maybe you could use King David as a memory cue.

## 3.3: Passage posers

Before you begin, cover the text on the opposite page. Now read the following text, taken from *Dracula* by Bram Stoker, one or two times through. Then, continue opposite.

'3 May. Bistritz. – Left Munich at 8:35 pm, on 1st May, arriving at Vienna early next morning; should have arrived at 6:46, but train was an hour late. Buda-Pesth seems a wonderful place, from the glimpse which I got of it from the train and the little I could walk through the streets. I feared to go very far from the station, as we had arrived late and would start as near the correct time as possible. The impression I had was that we were leaving the West and entering the East; the most western of splendid bridges over the Danube, which is here of noble width and depth, took us among the traditions of Turkish rule.

We left in pretty good time, and came after nightfall to Klausenburgh. Here I stopped for the night at the Hotel Royale. I had for dinner, or rather supper, a chicken done up some way with red pepper, which was very good but thirsty. (Memorandum: get recipe for Mina). I asked the waiter, and he said it was called "paprika hendl," and that, as it was a national dish, I should be able to get it anywhere along the Carpathians. I found my smattering of German very useful here; indeed, I don't know how I should be able to get on without it.'

# *Recall*

Now cover the opposite page. Can you answer the following questions about the extract from *Dracula* that you have just read?

1.  On what date was the diary entry written?

2.  At what time did the writer say they left Munich?

3.  How late was the train arriving into Vienna?

4.  Which river does the writer describe as having 'splendid bridges'?

5.  What is the name of the hotel the writer stayed in?

6.  Who did the writer intend to obtain a recipe for?

7.  Which mountain range does the writer mention, in reference to the dish he ate?

8.  Which language did the writer mention they 'have a smattering of'?

## 3.4: Winning words

First, cover everything below the dividing line on this page. Then, study this list of winners of Best Picture at the Oscars, listed (reading down first) in reverse chronological order of win, until you think you have memorized them. Once you're ready, cover up the list and reveal the instructions below.

| | |
|---|---|
| **Nomadland** | **Titanic** |
| **Parasite** | **Braveheart** |
| **Moonlight** | **Unforgiven** |
| **Spotlight** | **Platoon** |
| **Argo** | **Amadeus** |
| **Crash** | **Gandhi** |
| **Chicago** | **Rocky** |
| **Gladiator** | **Patton** |

## Recall

Can you recall all of the movies?

...........................................................................................................................

...........................................................................................................................

...........................................................................................................................

...........................................................................................................................

...........................................................................................................................

...........................................................................................................................

...........................................................................................................................

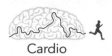
Cardio

## Master manipulator

You have already been introduced to strategies for
visuospatial short-term memory and mental rotation tasks.
Remember that you can use verbalization to transform visual
to verbal information, rotate parts of an object at a time
or choose a holistic approach, chunk parts of the image to
reduce memory load, or combine these types of strategies
to get even better results. Here, you have the opportunity
to build on these skills further. You might want to observe
your use of strategies as you tackle these tasks. What is your
preferred strategy? How does this depend on the type of
task? Use the space below to make a note of your strategies.

_____

_____

_____

_____

_____

_____

_____

_____

_____

## 3.5: *Odd one out*

Which of the images, A to E, is the odd one out from each set – and why?

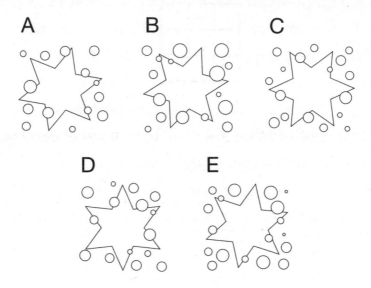

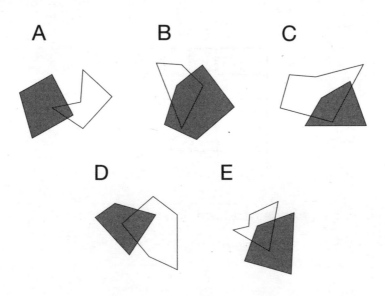

# 3.6: Squaring up

How many squares of all sizes (1×1, 2×2 and so on) can you count in total in this grid?

Now what about with this 4×4 grid? How many squares of all sizes can you count?

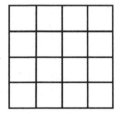

Finally, how about with this 5×5 grid? How many squares of all sizes can you count now?

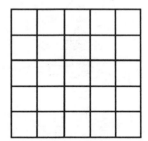

Can you work out a general method of calculating the number of squares in a square grid of any size, x by x?

# 3.7: *Building blocks*

In each of the puzzles below, which set of blocks – A to D – can be rearranged to form the assembly shown? All blocks must be used exactly once each.

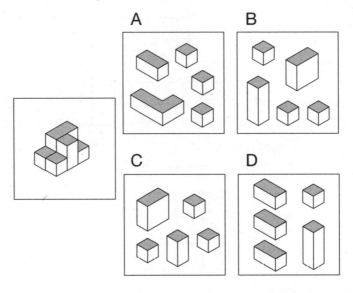

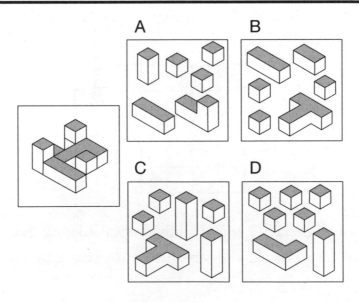

# 3.8: Cube counting

How many cubes are there in each of the following images? Each began as a 4×4×4 block before some cubes were removed. None of the cubes are 'floating' in mid-air.

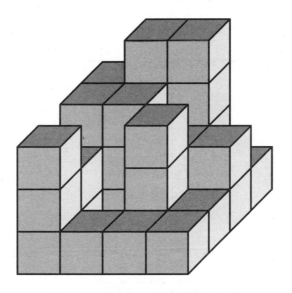

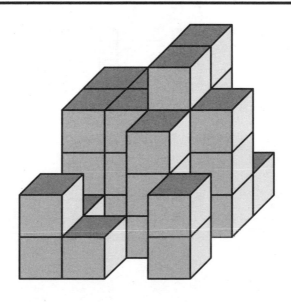

POINTS

# 3.9: Grid memory

Look at the pattern in the first grid on the left of the page, then cover it over and see if you can accurately reproduce it in the empty grid to its right. Repeat similarly for the second grid.

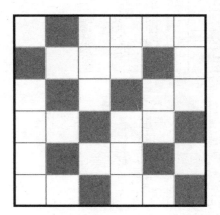 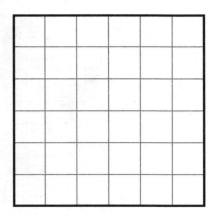

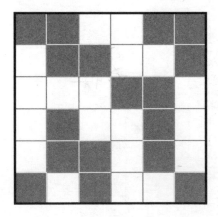 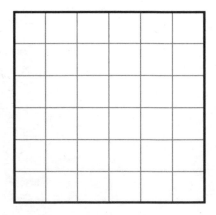

# 3.10: Hidden image

Which of the options, A to D, conceals the image shown on the far left of each puzzle? It may be rotated but all elements of it must be visible.

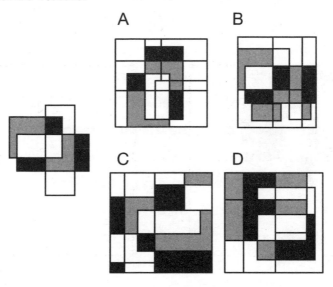

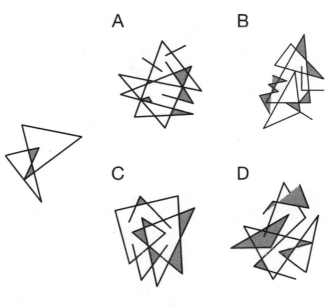

## The art of deduction

Deduction allows us to draw specific conclusions from general facts about the world, which we will here refer to as premises. Many examples of numerical reasoning and logic you encounter in standard puzzle games or during your school years involve this type of reasoning. Sudoku, for instance, has as its first premise that every row and every square contain each number between 1 and 9 only once. That is the general rule of the game that applies to each example. For each individual sudoku puzzle, other premises depend on the numbers that are given to you in the beginning. Based on these rules, you then deduce which numbers belong where. This top-down approach is at the core of deductive reasoning: going from a general rule to derive specific conclusions.

## 3.11: Black-out sudoku

Place a digit from 1 to 9 into every empty white square so that no digit repeats in any row, column or bold-lined 3×3 box. Shaded squares must remain empty. Be careful, however, since they will not always 'represent' the same digit in each of their row, column and 3×3 box.

| 6 | 1 |   | 7 | 9 |   | ▓ | 8 | 4 |
|   |   | 7 |   |   | 4 |   |   | 3 |
|   |   |   | ▓ | 5 | 3 |   | 7 |   |
|   | 5 | 6 |   | 4 | ▓ | 9 |   | 8 |
| 2 |   | ▓ | 5 |   | 1 | 7 |   | 6 |
| 7 |   | 3 |   | 8 |   | 1 | 5 | ▓ |
|   | ▓ |   | 9 | 2 | 8 |   |   |   |
| 9 |   |   | 4 |   |   | 5 | ▓ | 2 |
| 8 | 7 |   |   | ▓ | 5 |   | 9 | 1 |

# 3.12: Number pyramid

Write a number in each empty block, so that every block (above the bottom level) is equal to the sum of the two blocks directly beneath it.

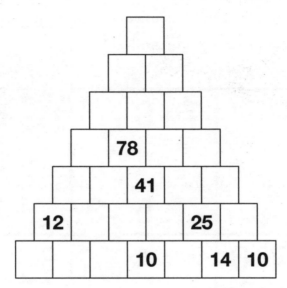

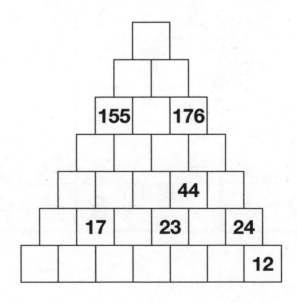

# 3.13: Jigdoku

Complete this jigdoku puzzle by placing a letter from A to G into each empty square, so that no letter repeats in any row, column or bold-lined jigsaw shape.

# The art of deduction (continued)

Can we do the same for verbal reasoning? Let's look at an example.

▶ Premise 1: Londoners live in England.

▶ Premise 2: England is part of the United Kingdom.

Assuming that both of these statements are true, we can say with absolute certainty that Londoners live in the UK.

Within the framework of this logical problem, let's say someone now told you they met some English guy in a pub. They conclude from this that the man must have been a Londoner. Unless they actually asked him to verify, you can point out that they simply cannot be sure that their conclusion is true. You can then smugly add that this is a typical example of overgeneralization without verification.

Deductive reasoning is used all the time by mathematicians and scientists, but it was also what you would have used in the train example from Chapter 2: the fact that the train will arrive in ten minutes is Premise 1. Your knowledge that it takes you no less than twelve minutes on foot to the train station (even if you run) is Premise 2. The conclusion that you cannot get there on time if you go on foot therefore *must* be true.

Cardio

# Elementary

Real life is often messy and you may not know if a general premise is definitely correct. When that is the case inductive reasoning may help you find out whether specific observations you make in everyday life can be used to draw a general conclusion about the world:

▶ you see a dog in the park and it lets you pet it;

▶ you see a dog sitting next to an infant without harming the child;

▶ you keep on encountering dogs in many positive situations and you conclude that dogs are friendly, nice to be around and won't hurt you.

However, that conclusion does not necessarily have to be true based on the evidence you have accumulated, rather it *may* be true. If you then hear about a dog biting the postman, this does not mean that your conclusion about dogs is entirely false. It simply means, *most* but not all dogs are friendly.

Inductive reasoning therefore does not provide certainty, only likely conclusions. It follows a bottom-up approach going from specific examples to general rules – the opposite of what you do in deductive reasoning. The more observations you make of dogs, the more confident you can

be in your hypothesis that dogs tend to be friendly towards humans.

You employ inductive reasoning constantly, simply by using observations from the past to predict the future. This is effective because the rules that led to events in the past are often still valid in the future.

However, inductive reasoning also has its pitfalls. Sometimes, the future cannot simply be predicted from the past. Importantly though, your specific experience of the past is defined by your preconception which will colour your conclusions and predictions. Biases are quite normal, we're all human after all and working with a limited set of knowledge and experience.

But what should you do if you hope to confront your biases? Be like Sherlock Holmes, who famously said: 'When you have eliminated the impossible, whatever remains, however improbable, must be the truth.' Simply put, this means looking at all the evidence and before jumping to conclusions, determine whether there may be multiple possible explanations or solutions to a problem. This may not always be the most obvious one.

If possible, seek other means of gathering more information and, step by step, strike out options that are incompatible with all the 'data' you have collected. In the end, choose the one option that is most likely to be true.

Devising puzzles for this type of reasoning is challenging, so the best way to get into this logical mindset is to apply it to an observation in real life for which an explanation is not obvious; or use it for a complex problem in school, work, or elsewhere in life.

For now, you can continue with the following pages with more abstract visuospatial reasoning tasks. They combine aspects of inductive and deductive reasoning as you follow patterns and infer rules.

# 3.14: What's missing?

The eight boxes below contain eight steps in a logical sequence which has been jumbled out of order. One of the boxes is empty, however. Draw the correct picture in it.

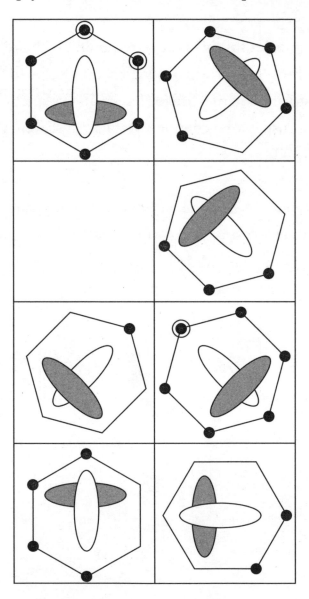

# 3.15: Complete the sequence

Which of the options, A to E, should be placed in the empty box on each top row in order to create a logical sequence?

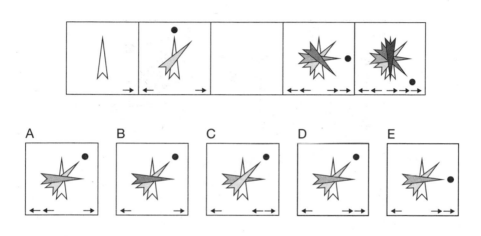

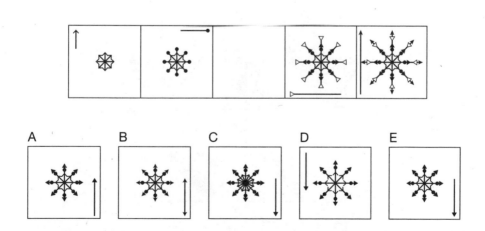

## 3.16: Complete the square

Which of the four options, A to D, should be placed into the empty square in each grid to complete the pattern?

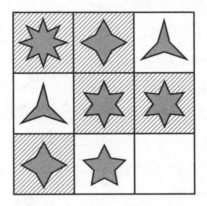

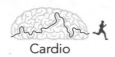
Cardio

## Beyond the pages

For many people, their everyday lives, be it leisure or work, do not provide many opportunities for creative thinking. And that's a shame, because being creative, coming up with something completely new, is incredibly rewarding and a way in which you keep your brain from trotting along its tried and tested path. Even in the later years at school, teaching and learning are mostly focused on fact learning, or logic and reasoning, with answers to tests often being either right or wrong. Let's break that mould. And for some of the following examples, let's also break out of these pages for a while.

POINTS

## *3.17: Writing practice*

Grab a notepad and pen, then try recalling a recent memory which involved another person and rewrite that memory from their perspective, adding in thoughts that that person might have had in the moment.

▶ Why did they act the way they did?

▶ What are their goals?

▶ What did they think of about you in that moment and why?

## 3.18: Time traveller

Imagine how a time traveler from the middle ages – or from the Roman Empire if you prefer – would describe our inventions and way of life.

▶ What would surprise them?

▶ What would they find ridiculous?

▶ What goes against their own morals?

▶ How would they try to explain our world to a person from their time who has never seen anything from our future?

Grab a notepad and pen and write as much as you can.

## 3.19: Transport designer

Experiment with using your visual creativity by seeing if you can draw a design for a new means of transport. It can involve any method of movement you like.

Use a blank sheet of paper for this challenge.

## Beyond the pages (continued)

To some, it may seem nonsensical to engage in exercises such as **'3.18: Time traveller' on page 138**: what good do they do? Quite a bit actually:

▶ you now know that novel experiences are a great tool to challenge your brain and create new connections;

▶ you become more accustomed to generating lots of new ideas;

▶ you are actively engaging your cognitive processes to *do* something rather than just passively taking in information;

▶ you learn to judge yourself less (as illustrated in the previous chapter);

▶ hopefully, you're also having fun while doing so.

Getting yourself in the habit of not following habits can be quite challenging and may sound contradictory. Yet, it simply means becoming more comfortable trying something new and challenging your preconceptions. A brain which is given the opportunity of varied experiences will naturally have more different pieces of information from which it can draw to generate novel ideas and solve complex problems.

Finally, it helps to remember that the best path forward to tackling complex problems often entails a combination of divergent thinking, which uses creativity to generate novel ideas, and convergent thinking, which uses logical reasoning to critically evaluate these ideas. Use your logic but challenge your preconceptions and make sure you are not leaving out unusual ideas. Hopefully, after you had the opportunity to engage in this type of thinking more frequently within these pages, you give yourself more freedom to approach situations in real life with this type of mindset in the future.

# 3.20: About the house

Spend as long as you think you need studying *the order of* this list of rooms that might be found in a house. Once you think you have memorized the list, turn the page and follow the instructions. You will only be asked to recall the order they were listed, not the rooms themselves.

1. **Kitchen**
2. **Study**
3. **Lounge**
4. **Bathroom**
5. **Living Room**
6. **Basement**
7. **Utility**
8. **Garage**
9. **Bedroom**
10. **Library**
11. **Nursery**
12. **Closet**
13. **Porch**
14. **Hallway**
15. **Attic**
16. **Larder**
17. **Cloakroom**
18. **Workshop**

# Recall (continued from previous page)

The same list of rooms has now been rearranged into alphabetical order. Can you write a number next to each room below, to show its original position in the list on the previous page?

........... **Attic**
........... **Basement**
........... **Bathroom**
........... **Bedroom**
........... **Cloakroom**
........... **Closet**
........... **Garage**
........... **Hallway**
........... **Kitchen**
........... **Larder**
........... **Library**
........... **Living Room**
........... **Lounge**
........... **Nursery**
........... **Porch**
........... **Study**
........... **Utility**
........... **Workshop**

# 3.21: Shape link

Draw a series of separate paths, each connecting a pair of identical shapes. No more than one path can enter any square, and paths can only travel horizontally or vertically between squares.

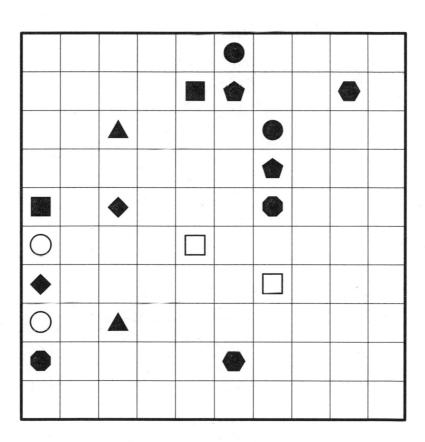

# 3.22: *Tracing paper*

Which of the options, A to D, represents the view of each image shown to the left when folded in half along the dashed line? Assume it has been drawn on transparent paper.

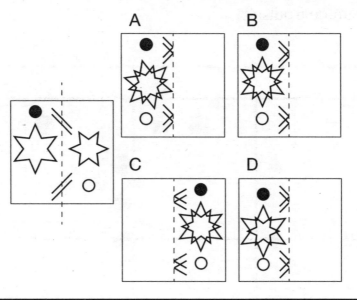

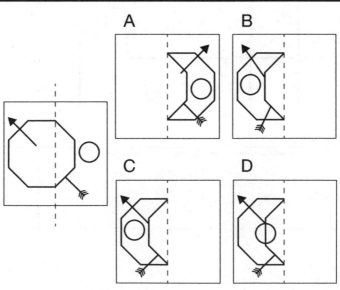

# 3.23: Careful counting

How many rectangles and squares – of any size – can you count in the following picture? There are more than you might think, and don't forget to include the shape that runs all around the outside!

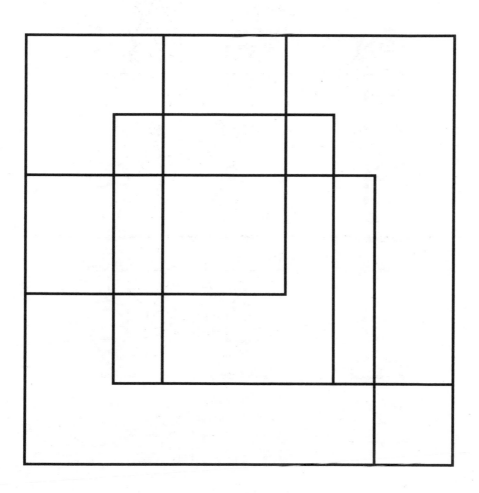

# 3.24: Face off

Start by covering the page opposite. Then, spend two minutes studying these names and faces. Once you think you've memorized which name goes with which face, cover up this page and read the instructions opposite.

Megan     Dave     Rita

Jack     Elizabeth     Oliver

Ally     Phoebe     Tim

# Recall (continued from previous page)

All but three of the faces from the opposite page are shown again here. Can you first fill in the gap beneath the faces with the correct names, then use the spaces at the bottom to write in the names of the three missing faces?

_____

_____

_____

_____

_____

_____

_____

_____

_____

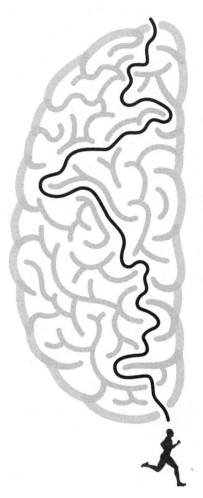

# 4.

# COOLING

# DOWN

## *Cooling down*

After any intense physical exercise, ending with a restorative stretch and a cool-down is essential. For your brain exercises, finishing with some simpler puzzles will keep you from getting too discouraged if the more challenging exercises were frustrating at times and if you found it difficult to progress. These puzzles will remind you of your solid basic cognitive skill set.

The cool-down will also provide you with a chance to reflect on your experiences during tasks you found most challenging: what was it that went well? What was particularly difficult? Taking some notes on where you were proud of yourself and where you would like to take it next can help structure your next puzzle session and keep you motivated. It will also help you identify the types of strategies you may want to practice more. You can use **'Your progress notes' on page 188** for this, if you wish.

You have now read a great deal about various types of puzzles and a cool-down is a relaxing way to round up your practice. Rather than making you learn new strategies or touting more health advice, this chapter includes some of the fascinating stories of the people who inadvertently led neuroscientists to uncover some of the mysteries of the brain.

## Learning from patients

We often learn better when we are presented with stories rather than dry facts. The stories of these patients are tragic, yet intriguing, and because our brains tend to better remember information with emotional content, they also happen to be an effective vehicle for knowledge about the organization of the human brain. Until the advent of neuroimaging methods that now allow scientists to study the brains of healthy, awake humans while they perform tasks in a brain scanner, there was only one way to map the functions of specific brain regions in humans: observing the behaviour of patients who were unfortunate enough to suffer from medical conditions or accidents that damaged a part of their brain. Despite the challenges and often suffering these and many other patients had to endure because of their injuries, their contributions to cognitive neuroscience remain their legacy.

Brain regions located all the way at the back of your head are the first to receive visual information from the eyes. From there, different regions process information about an object's identity, while others contain spatial information about that object's position in the environment and yet others combine this information at later stages in the visual processing hierarchy. This characteristic organization of visual

information processing can lead to seemingly odd patterns of behaviour when certain regions of the brain are injured. For instance, patient D.F., with damage to parts of the processing stream for object recognition, could catch a ball but was unable to name or copy a picture of an apple.

## Blindsighted

Even more fascinating is what researchers refer to as *blindsight*. Some patients with damage to early visual brain areas become unconscious of objects in their visual field, leading to a form of blindness where their eyes see but their consciousness does not. In case you really want to show off, you can remember this condition under the term 'agnosopsia': not knowing or being ignorant to what one sees. If you held up an apple to one such patient and asked them what object you were holding at that moment, they would not even know you were holding anything at all, let alone be capable of naming the object. And yet, in many cases these patients still retain the ability to correctly move their eyes to look at or even point to that object. These surprising medical cases eerily show how information outside our awareness can still guide our actions, raising interesting questions about the nature of human consciousness which neuroscientists have yet to answer.

# 4.1: Top-down problem

Which of the options, A to D, represents the view of each 3D object when seen from the direction of the arrow?

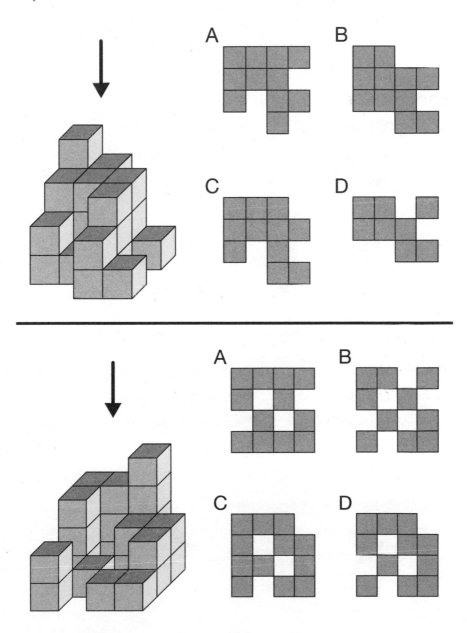

153

## 4.2: Reflect on this

Imagine reflecting each of these two images in the dashed lines shown. Which lower image, A to D, then results in each case? Ignore the changes in scale.

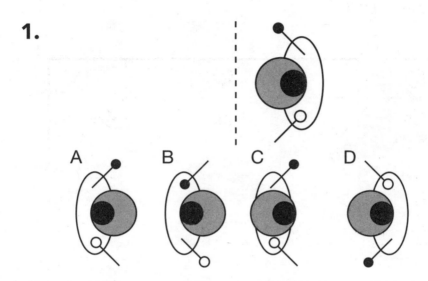

**1.**

A    B    C    D

**2.**

A    B    C    D

# 4.3: Shape link

Draw a series of separate paths, each connecting a pair of identical shapes. No more than one path can enter any square, and paths can only travel horizontally or vertically between squares.

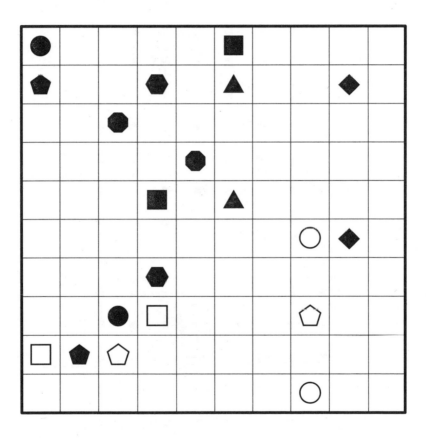

# 4.4: Fences

Draw horizontal and vertical lines to join all of the dots in each grid into a single loop which visits every dot exactly once, and does not cross itself.

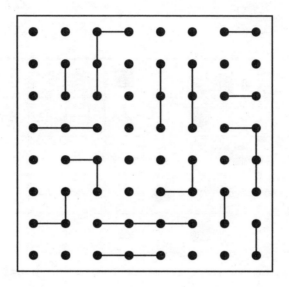

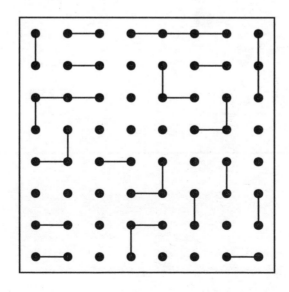

# 4.5: Fold and punch

Imagine folding and then punching paper as shown in each of the two puzzles. Unfold, and which image, A to D, results?

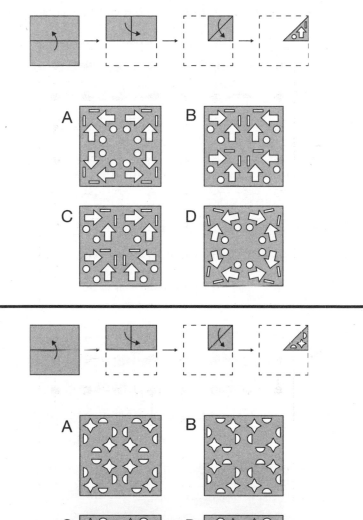

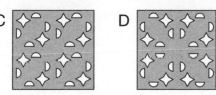

# Caught in the present

The most famous patient with a brain lesion was H.M.
(now known as Henry Molaison) whose treatment for
medication-resistant epilepsy consisted of the removal of
the  hippocampus, the brain region doctors later found to
be necessary to form long-term memories for personally
experienced events and new knowledge. H.M. was the most
prominent case of anterograde amnesia: new information
was lost to him as were recent memories from his life prior
to surgery, yet his older memories, language and knowledge
acquired prior to the operation, remained. His ability to learn
new facts had almost entirely disappeared, but he could
acquire novel motor skills and maintained above average
intelligence.

Even more tragic than the case of H.M. is that of Clive
Wearing, a professional musician whose brain was damaged
by a severe case of herpes simplex infection causing lesions
including regions in the same brain area that was removed
in H.M. Not only did Clive have anterograde amnesia like
H.M., where new memories cannot be formed, he also had
retrograde amnesia, being unable to recall most memories
from his life prior to the infection.

Also called '30-second Clive', Wearing was caught in a perpetual feeling of having just awoken from a coma, with his life being largely constrained to the contents of his short-term memory which never made it into to his long-term memory. The connections between his short-term buffer and his archives for facts and personally experienced events were essentially severed. Although Clive had forgotten the names of his children, he remembered the love he felt for his wife and would joyously greet her every time she returned to the same room, even if she had only been gone briefly. He retained the ability to learn new motor skills and remained capable of playing complex musical pieces even though he could not recall their titles or composers. These remarkable cases of memory damage and maintenance demonstrate a divide between learning factual information and utilizing or acquiring motor skills, as well as between the recall of old memories and the formation of novel ones.

# 4.6: A gem of a challenge

First, cover everything below the dividing line on this page. Then, spend a few minutes memorizing this list of precious stones. Once you're ready, cover up the list and reveal the instructions below.

| | |
|---|---|
| Ruby | Moonstone |
| Beryl | Pearl |
| Sapphire | Opal |
| Peridot | Emerald |
| Onyx | Topaz |
| Jet | Coral |
| Garnet | Diamond |

# Recall

Can you now write out the list of gemstones again? To help you, the final letter of each stone has been provided, although they are listed in reverse order to that given above.

| | |
|---|---|
| ..............d | ..............t |
| ..............l | ..............t |
| ..............z | ..............x |
| ..............d | ..............t |
| ..............l | ..............e |
| ..............l | ..............l |
| ..............e | ..............y |

# 4.7: Grid memory

Look at the pattern in the first grid on the left of the page, then cover it over and see if you can accurately reproduce it in the empty grid to its right. Repeat similarly for the second and third grids.

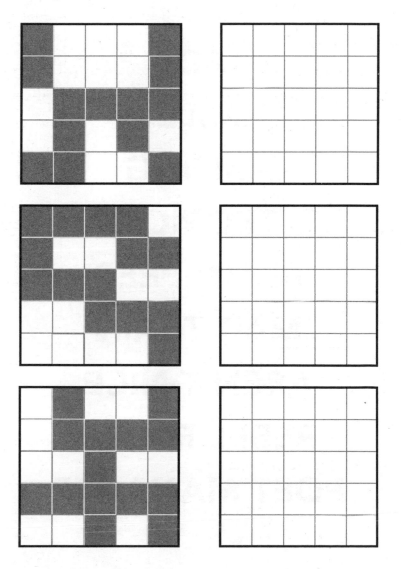

## 4.8: *Fruity finding*

How quickly can you unscramble the names of these fruits? All of the names are one word in length. Each fruit's name is a single word, so ignore any spaces or punctuation in the anagrams.

## TADE

## MILE

## AMONG

## TROPICA

## PLAIN PEEP

## MAD TRAIN

## AREN'T NICE

## REBEL RYDER

## POET MANAGER

## 4.9: Musical memory

First, cover everything below the dividing line on this page. Then, spend a few minutes memorizing this list of musical instruments. Then, once you're ready, cover up the list and reveal the instructions below.

| | |
|---|---|
| **Guitar** | **Oboe** |
| **Sitar** | **Tuba** |
| **Harmonica** | **Violin** |
| **Saxophone** | **Harp** |
| **Timpani** | **Bugle** |
| **Glockenspiel** | **Double bass** |
| **Mandolin** | **Piano** |

## Recall

Can you now write out the list of instruments again? To help you, the final letter of each instrument has been provided, although the list is in a different order to that given above.

| | |
|---|---|
| **B**.................................. | **O**.................................. |
| **D**.................................. | **P**.................................. |
| **G**.................................. | **S**.................................. |
| **G**.................................. | **S**.................................. |
| **H**.................................. | **T**.................................. |
| **H**.................................. | **T**.................................. |
| **M**.................................. | **V**.................................. |

## 4.10: Literary recall

Before you begin, cover the text on the opposite page. Now read the following text, taken from *Little Women* by Louisa May Alcott, one or two times. Then, continue opposite.

'Christmas won't be Christmas without any presents,' grumbled Jo, lying on the rug.

'It's so dreadful to be poor!' sighed Meg, looking down at her old dress.

'I don't think it's fair for some girls to have plenty of pretty things, and other girls nothing at all,' added little Amy, with an injured sniff.

'We've got Father and Mother, and each other,' said Beth contentedly from her corner.

The four young faces on which the firelight shone brightened at the cheerful words, but darkened again as Jo said sadly, 'We haven't got Father, and shall not have him for a long time.' She didn't say 'perhaps never,' but each silently added it, thinking of Father far away, where the fighting was.

# *Recall*

Now cover the opposite page. The text below is almost identical to the original you have just read, but not quite. Can you identify which ten words have been changed?

'Christmas won't be Christmas without any gifts,' grumbled Jo, lying on the carpet.

'It's so awful to be poor!' sighed Meg, looking down at her old skirt.

'I don't think it's fair for some girls to have plenty of lovely things, and other girls nothing at all,' added little Amy, with an unhappy sniff.

'We've got Father and Mother, and each other,' said Beth reassuringly from her corner.

The four youthful faces on which the firelight shone brightened at the cheerful words, but fell again as Jo said sadly, 'We haven't got Father, and shall not have him for a long time.' She didn't say 'perhaps never,' but each silently added it, thinking of Father far away, where the war was.

# 4.11: Password posers

Start by covering up everything below the dividing line, then spend up to a minute memorizing these six codes and passwords. Once time is up, reveal the text beneath.

| | |
|---|---|
| **Bank card PIN:** | **1290** |
| **Email password:** | **Mail44** |
| **Computer login:** | **H4RDdr1v3** |
| **Internet access:** | **hom3OnLiNe** |
| **Voicemail PIN:** | **101012** |
| **Family cloud:** | **BakerPhotos2022** |

## Recall

Cover over the top part of the page. Then, can you fill in the gaps below with the codes and passwords you remember? They are in a different order to above.

**Voicemail PIN:** .................................................

**Computer login:** .................................................

**Email password:** .................................................

**Internet access:** .................................................

**Bank card PIN:** .................................................

**Family cloud:** .................................................

## Back to the future

It is not just recalling the past and making new memories of the present that are impaired in patients with hippocampal damage. In more recent years, studies have also found that patients with amnesia caused by hippocampal lesions struggle with creative thinking and conjuring up future scenarios. Why might that be? Creative thinking demands the rapid recombination of the contents of our knowledge and memory to imagine new scenarios. We use the elements available to us from what we have learned to do so. Without our librarian granting us access to these memories, there is little material to work with. This is also why this book encourages you to seek novel experiences as fodder for your imagination. Unfortunately, for many patients with severe hippocampal damage, mental time travel into the past and into the future becomes more difficult or even impossible. They are quite literally caught in the present.

## Don't panic!

You might find that it is nearly or completely impossible for you to conjure up mental images in the creativity or memory tasks. Don't panic! It doesn't mean you have hippocampal damage. If it so happens that you generally cannot form images in your mind's eye at all, then you may have aphantasia – the inability to create mental imagery.

Many aphantasics are simply born this way, don't even know that they lack this ability and go through life completely normally. They develop other means to recall visual information by translating images into words, showing once again how dynamic and flexible the brain is in using different strategies to succeed and how combining both verbal and visual memory strategies provides you with a more versatile cognitive toolkit.

Now try the creative puzzle on the following page.

## 4.12: Object-ive thinking

How many unusual uses can you think of for each of the objects listed below? Write down as many as you can think of, and try to avoid including anything that the object in question would 'normally' be used for.

# Fishing net

..................................................................................................

..................................................................................................

..................................................................................................

..................................................................................................

# Curved door handle

..................................................................................................

..................................................................................................

..................................................................................................

..................................................................................................

## Who's in the driver's seat?

For decades, researchers believed the frontal regions of the brain (those right behind your forehead) to be 'cognitively silent' because damage to or removal of tissue in these areas did not necessarily result in significant losses of a person's mental faculties. But over time it became apparent that these patients experienced changes in their behaviour and, disturbingly, even their personality.

The most prominent of these cases was Phineas Gage. In 1848, the railroad worker Gage had a life-changing accident in which an explosion sent an iron rod 43 inches long and 1.25 inches wide upward through his skull damaging the frontal part of his brain. Astonishingly, immediately after the injury, Gage got up and walked normally. What's more, the doctor who examined him did not even find any cognitive or behavioural abnormalities. However, following the damage to his brain, Gage became notably impulsive, often making plans but quickly abandoning them, and engaging in socially inappropriate behaviour. He also could no longer keep a job, even though he was an excellent employee prior to his accident.

The case of Phineas Gage – and many other patients with similar injuries – helped neuroscientists learn that these

frontal brain regions are crucial for executive processes, the set of functions we have been referring to in this book as the 'architect' because they support planning actions to meet a goal while inhibiting unsuitable actions or habits, and adapting to new challenges by learning new behaviours. Working memory functions also rely on these regions and their widespread pathways of communication with other brain areas. Similarly, keeping focus to crack a demanding logical reasoning task also requires these regions to ignore distractions and inhibit urges to give up and instead relax while watching TV on your couch. This explains Gage's difficulties to inhibit unsuitable behaviours and stick to his plans.

## 4.13: Dominoes

Draw along the dashed lines to divide this grid into a complete set of dominoes, from 0-0 up to 6-6. Each domino will appear exactly once, so use the cross-off chart to keep track of which dominoes have been placed.

| 2 | 5 | 1 | 6 | 3 | 6 | 4 | 4 |
|---|---|---|---|---|---|---|---|
| 2 | 6 | 6 | 3 | 5 | 6 | 2 | 1 |
| 0 | 3 | 2 | 3 | 0 | 6 | 2 | 0 |
| 4 | 4 | 5 | 2 | 1 | 0 | 3 | 4 |
| 5 | 3 | 1 | 1 | 0 | 1 | 4 | 1 |
| 2 | 0 | 4 | 3 | 3 | 5 | 6 | 5 |
| 2 | 6 | 5 | 5 | 1 | 4 | 0 | 0 |

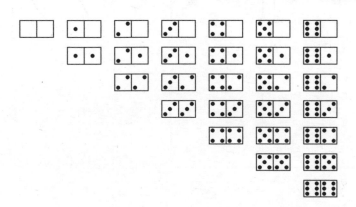

## 4.14: *Crack the code*

Crack the code used to describe each image, and pick which option, 'a' to 'd', should replace the question mark.

**AVCK**

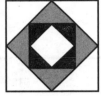

**JODU**

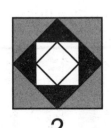

**?**

a. JVDU   b. AVCU

c. AVDU   d. AOCK

**JVCU**

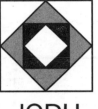

**JOCK**

---

**EFGJ**

**EQGR**

**?**

a. YQZR   b. YFGR

c. YQGJ   d. EFZR

**EQZR**

**YFZR**

## 4.15: Sudoku

Complete this sudoku puzzle by placing a digit from 1 to 9 into each empty square, so that no digit repeats in any row, column or bold-lined 3×3 box.

| 5 |   |   |   |   |   |   |   |   |
|---|---|---|---|---|---|---|---|---|
|   | 8 | 7 | 5 |   |   |   | 1 |   |
|   | 3 |   | 6 | 4 |   |   |   |   |
| 8 |   |   |   |   |   |   |   | 6 |
|   |   | 4 | 3 |   | 5 | 2 |   |   |
| 9 |   |   |   |   |   |   |   | 3 |
|   |   |   |   | 5 | 3 |   | 4 |   |
|   | 6 |   |   |   | 1 | 7 | 2 |   |
|   |   |   |   |   |   |   |   | 8 |

## Happy ending

So, what happened to poor Phineas in the end? Reports from many years after his accident suggest that he must have managed to use his remaining frontal lobe regions to slowly adapt to his new circumstances. He even managed to hold down a long-term job. His story shows us the brain's astonishing potential for recovery and re-organization.

## Only the beginning of the adventure

Hopefully your journey through this book aided your brain in some re-organization by learning new facts, adapting your thinking, and utilizing new strategies to become a better puzzler.

If you have made it this far, congratulations on your stamina and willpower! Now it is up to you to keep your momentum going and carry what you have learned into your everyday life.

Try to apply the tips and tricks presented to you here beyond the confines of these pages. That is the secret to reaping long-term benefits of all your hard work.

Your brain will thank you for it.

# 4.16: What's missing?

The eight boxes below contain eight steps in a logical sequence which has been jumbled out of order. One of the boxes is empty, however. Draw the correct picture in it.

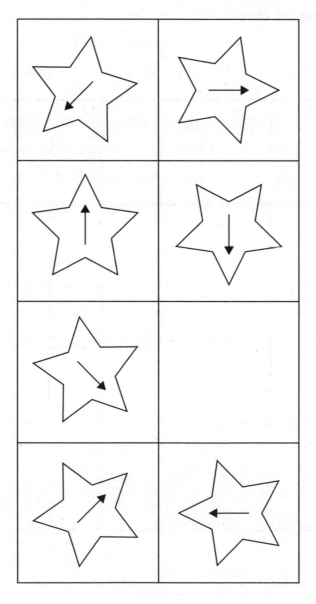

# 4.17: Careful counting

How many rectangles and squares – of any size – can you count in the following picture? There are more than you might think, and don't forget to include the shape that runs all around the outside!

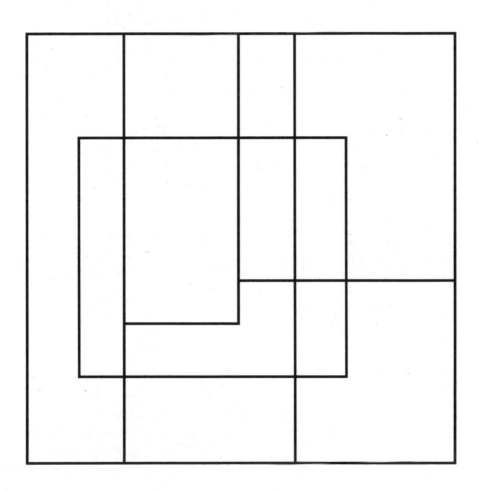

# Solutions

## 1.2: Country confusion

- ▶ PERU
- ▶ TONGA
- ▶ ISRAEL
- ▶ ALGERIA
- ▶ NORWAY
- ▶ ECUADOR
- ▶ PORTUGAL
- ▶ ARGENTINA
- ▶ CAMEROON
- ▶ SWITZERLAND

## 1.3 Sudoku 6×6

| 6 | 3 | 1 | 2 | 4 | 5 |
|---|---|---|---|---|---|
| 2 | 5 | 4 | 6 | 3 | 1 |
| 5 | 1 | 6 | 3 | 2 | 4 |
| 3 | 4 | 2 | 5 | 1 | 6 |
| 1 | 6 | 3 | 4 | 5 | 2 |
| 4 | 2 | 5 | 1 | 6 | 3 |

| 3 | 5 | 4 | 6 | 2 | 1 |
|---|---|---|---|---|---|
| 6 | 2 | 1 | 5 | 4 | 3 |
| 4 | 3 | 5 | 1 | 6 | 2 |
| 2 | 1 | 6 | 3 | 5 | 4 |
| 1 | 6 | 2 | 4 | 3 | 5 |
| 5 | 4 | 3 | 2 | 1 | 6 |

## 1.4: Dominoes

| 2 | 0 | 4 | 4 | 0 | 4 |
|---|---|---|---|---|---|
| 3 | 2 | 1 | 3 | 0 | 2 |
| 2 | 4 | 1 | 3 | 2 | 2 |
| 0 | 0 | 3 | 1 | 4 | 0 |
| 3 | 1 | 4 | 1 | 1 | 3 |

| 3 | 3 | 2 | 4 | 2 | 2 |
|---|---|---|---|---|---|
| 3 | 3 | 1 | 4 | 0 | 0 |
| 1 | 1 | 2 | 4 | 1 | 4 |
| 1 | 3 | 0 | 0 | 1 | 4 |
| 0 | 4 | 2 | 3 | 2 | 0 |

## 1.5: Travel network

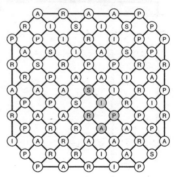

## 1.6: Odd one out

- ▶ E – this is the only image with 6, not 5, ellipses
- ▶ D – the black/white arrowhead has its colours flipped relative to the rest

## 1.7: Reflect on this

▶ C

▶ D

## 1.8: Shape link

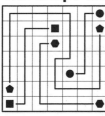

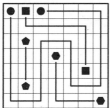

## 1.9: Top-down problem

▶ C

▶ A

## 1.11: Building blocks

▶ D

▶ C

## 1.12: Fold and punch

▶ B

▶ A

## 1.13: Password posers

▶ 1: 3971

▶ 2: diamond

▶ 3: office

▶ 4: 1

▶ 5: 24

▶ 6: bank card PIN

## 1.15: Grimm recall

The changes are:

▶ Country/citadel

▶ Fairies/pixies

▶ Fine/ridiculous

▶ Many/twenty

▶ Grieved/annoyed

▶ Gasping/giggling

▶ Little/hilarious

▶ River/waterfall

▶ Daughter/son

▶ Girl/boy

## 1.19: Number pyramid

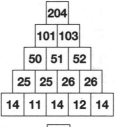

## 1.21: What's missing?

A segment is added and the image rotates 90° each step

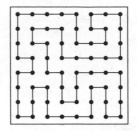

## 2.3: Shape link

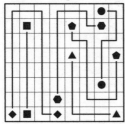

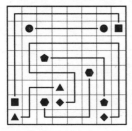

## 2.4: Fences

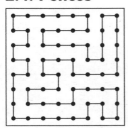

## 2.5: Hidden images

▶ C

▶ B

## 2.6: Tracing paper

▶ B

▶ D

## 2.7: Musical medleys

▶ MADONNA

▶ ELVIS PRESLEY

▶ STEVIE WONDER

▶ ELTON JOHN

▶ ED SHEERAN

▶ TAYLOR SWIFT

▶ DOLLY PARTON

▶ PAUL MCCARTNEY

## 2.8: A study in scarlet

The changes are:

▶ Difficult/hard

▶ Regular/predictable

▶ Breakfasted/eaten

▶ Chemical/biology

- City/town
- Seize/grab
- Sitting/living
- Vacant/empty

## 2.9: Shakespearean shakedown

- *As You Like It*
- *Much Ado About Nothing*
- *A Midsummer Night's Dream*
- *The Two Noble Kinsmen*
- *The Taming of the Shrew*
- *The Two Gentlemen of Verona*
- *All's Well that End's Well*
- *The Merry Wives of Windsor*

## 2.15: Sudoku

| 4 | 1 | 2 | 7 | 6 | 8 | 3 | 9 | 5 |
|---|---|---|---|---|---|---|---|---|
| 9 | 7 | 5 | 3 | 2 | 1 | 6 | 8 | 4 |
| 6 | 3 | 8 | 5 | 9 | 4 | 1 | 2 | 7 |
| 5 | 4 | 7 | 8 | 3 | 9 | 2 | 6 | 1 |
| 8 | 6 | 1 | 2 | 4 | 7 | 9 | 5 | 3 |
| 2 | 9 | 3 | 6 | 1 | 5 | 4 | 7 | 8 |
| 7 | 2 | 9 | 4 | 8 | 3 | 5 | 1 | 6 |
| 1 | 5 | 4 | 9 | 7 | 6 | 8 | 3 | 2 |
| 3 | 8 | 6 | 1 | 5 | 2 | 7 | 4 | 9 |

## 2.16: Number pyramid

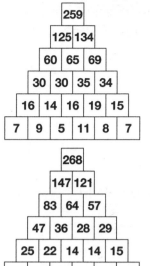

## 2.17: Crack the code

- c. ZRP
  - F = arrow points up
  - Z = arrow points down
  - Q = shaded large star
  - R = black large star
  - M = white large star
  - K = small star top right
  - P = small star bottom left
- b. RQX
  - W = pointed hexagon top
  - R = flat hexagon top
  - L = shaded triangle behind
  - Q = shaded triangle in front
  - X = white background
  - H = black background

## 2.18: Complete the sequence

▶ D. The black circle does not move. Moving left to right, a grey bar is added at each stage, with the group of bars moving clockwise around the square edges as the series progresses.

▶ A. Moving from left to right along the series, each frame is reflected relative to the previous square, and one new shape is added.

## 2.19: Complete the square

▶ A. Each row begins with a small square of a different shade, which is rotated 45° in each column moving rightwards. A second square is added behind it in the middle column, and then the duo is rotated in the rightmost column. Each row and column has exactly one of each shades for the small squares.

▶ C. Arrows point to the grid box with the next-higher number of black

circles. The circles are arranged randomly around the arrow, until it is covered by a ninth circle.

## 2.22: Cube counting

▶ 44 cubes

▶ 35 cubes

## 2.23: What's missing?

The black square snakes back and forth, leaving a fading trail. The entire image flips horizontally at each step.

## 3.2: Olympic scramble

▶ LUGE

▶ BIATHLON

▶ BADMINTON

▶ ATHLETICS

▶ SKELETON

▶ ROWING

▶ EQUESTRIAN

▶ SNOWBOARDING

▶ SKATEBOARDING

## 3.3 Passage posers

▶ 1: May 3rd

▶ 2: 8:35pm

▶ 3: An hour late

▶ 4: Danube

▶ 5: Hotel Royale

▶ 6: Mina

▶ 7: Carpathians

▶ 8: German

## 3.5: Odd one out

▶ C – the only star not overlapped by exactly 6 circles

▶ B – the grey shape has 5 sides, not 4, and the transparent shape has 4 sides, not 5

## 3.6: Squaring up

▶ 14 squares (9 1×1, 4 2×2 and 1 3×3)

▶ 30 squares (16 1×1, 9 2×2, 4 3×3 and 1 4×4)

▶ 55 squares (25 1×1, 16 2×2, 9 3×3 and 4 4×4 and 1 5×5)

▶ Take the sum of all square numbers from $1^2$ up to $x^2$, inclusive. Although it is not the intent of this question for you to derive the following, mathematically this is equivalent to evaluating: $( x (x+1) (2x+1) ) \div 6$

## 3.7: Building blocks

▶ C

▶ B

## 3.8: Cube counting

▶ 34 cubes

▶ 33 cubes

## 3.10: Hidden image

▶ A

▶ D

## 3.11: Black-out sudoku

| 6 | 1 | 5 | 7 | 9 | 2 |   | 8 | 4 |
|---|---|---|---|---|---|---|---|---|
|   | 9 | 7 | 8 | 6 | 4 | 2 | 1 | 3 |
| 4 | 2 | 8 |   | 5 | 3 | 6 | 7 | 9 |
| 1 | 5 | 6 | 2 | 4 |   | 9 | 3 | 8 |
| 2 | 8 |   | 5 | 3 | 1 | 7 | 4 | 6 |
| 7 | 4 | 3 | 6 | 8 | 9 | 1 | 5 |   |
| 5 |   | 4 | 9 | 2 | 8 | 3 | 6 | 7 |
| 9 | 3 | 1 | 4 | 7 | 6 | 5 |   | 2 |
| 8 | 7 | 2 | 3 |   | 5 | 4 | 9 | 1 |

## 3.12: Number pyramid

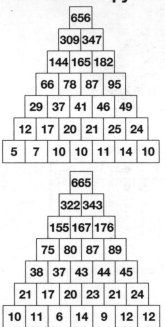

656

309 347

144 165 182

66 78 87 95

29 37 41 46 49

12 17 20 21 25 24

5 7 10 10 11 14 10

---

665

322 343

155 167 176

75 80 87 89

38 37 43 44 45

21 17 20 23 21 24

10 11 6 14 9 12 12

## 3.13: Jigdoku

| D | A | E | B | F | G | C |
|---|---|---|---|---|---|---|
| G | C | B | A | D | E | F |
| F | E | D | C | G | A | B |
| E | B | A | G | C | F | D |
| C | D | G | F | E | B | A |
| B | F | C | E | A | D | G |
| A | G | F | D | B | C | E |

## 3.14: What's missing?

At each step an extra circle is added to the perimeter, one corner clockwise from the previously added circle. When a second circle is added to an existing one,

a larger transparent circle is added on top. In addition, the entire image rotates 45° clockwise and the two ellipses change their stacking order back and forth at each step.

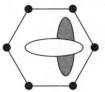

## 3.15: Complete the sequence

▶ D. A new central pointer shape is added at each stage reading from left to right; each new shape is shaded darker than the previous added shape, and laid on top. Small black dots appear in the space pointed to by the shape added in the previous frame. An arrow is added along the bottom of each frame, alternating between bottom right and bottom left placement.

▶ E. Reading from left to right across the frames, a new set of eight 'arrows' is added at each

stage, each increasing in size and pointing out from the centre of the arrangement. The style of arrow added at each stage is included in the corner of each frame, pointing to a different corner each time and moving clockwise around the frame.

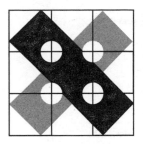

## 3.16: Complete the square

▶ D. The total number of points on all the stars in each row and column adds to 15. Also, stars with even numbers of points have a hatched background.

▶ C. A black rectangle is overlaid at 90° on top of a grey rectangle across the 9 squares, with four circular cut-out holes on the four central grid intersections. Also, every even-numbered square (reading left-to-right, top-bottom from 1 at the top-left) has been flipped horizontally. Without this flipping, the completed grid would look like this:

### 3.21: Shape link

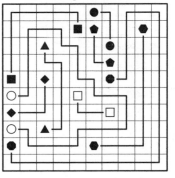

### 3.22: Tracing paper

▶ B

▶ C

### 3.23: Careful counting

There are 36 rectangles and squares in total

### 4.1: Top-down problem

▶ B

▶ D

## 4.2: Reflect on this

▶ A

▶ B

## 4.3: Shape link

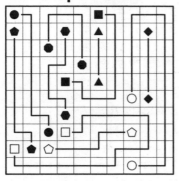

## 4.4 Fences

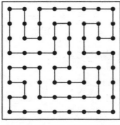

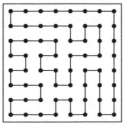

## 4.5 Fold and punch

▶ A

▶ D

## 4.8: Fruity finding

▶ DATE

▶ LIME

▶ MANGO

▶ APRICOT

▶ PINEAPPLE

▶ TAMARIND

▶ NECTARINE

▶ ELDERBERRY

▶ POMEGRANATE

## 4.10: Literary recall

The changes are:

▶ Presents/gifts

▶ Rug/carpet

▶ Dreadful/awful

▶ Dress/skirt

▶ Pretty/lovely

▶ Injured/unhappy

▶ Contentedly/reassuringly

▶ Young/youthful

▶ Darkened/fell

▶ Fighting/war

## 4.13: Dominoes

| 2 | 5 | 1 | 6 | 3 | 6 | 4 | 4 |
|---|---|---|---|---|---|---|---|
| 2 | 6 | 6 | 3 | 5 | 6 | 2 | 1 |
| 0 | 3 | 2 | 3 | 0 | 6 | 2 | 0 |
| 4 | 4 | 5 | 2 | 1 | 0 | 3 | 4 |
| 5 | 3 | 1 | 1 | 0 | 1 | 4 | 1 |
| 2 | 0 | 4 | 3 | 3 | 5 | 6 | 5 |
| 2 | 6 | 5 | 5 | 1 | 4 | 0 | 0 |

## 4.14: Crack the code

▶ b. AVCU
   A = grey large square
   J = white large square
   O = grey large diamond
   V = black large diamond
   C = white small square
   D = black small square
   K = black small diamond
   U = white small diamond

▶ d. EFZR
   E = solid arrowhead
   Y = non-solid arrowhead
   Q = tail feathers
   F = no tail feathers
   G = grey oval
   Z = white oval
   R = oval in front
   J = oval behind

## 4.15: Sudoku

| 5 | 4 | 9 | 1 | 3 | 7 | 8 | 6 | 2 |
|---|---|---|---|---|---|---|---|---|
| 6 | 8 | 7 | 5 | 2 | 9 | 3 | 1 | 4 |
| 2 | 3 | 1 | 6 | 4 | 8 | 5 | 9 | 7 |
| 8 | 5 | 3 | 9 | 1 | 2 | 4 | 7 | 6 |
| 1 | 7 | 4 | 3 | 6 | 5 | 2 | 8 | 9 |
| 9 | 2 | 6 | 7 | 8 | 4 | 1 | 5 | 3 |
| 7 | 9 | 2 | 8 | 5 | 3 | 6 | 4 | 1 |
| 3 | 6 | 8 | 4 | 9 | 1 | 7 | 2 | 5 |
| 4 | 1 | 5 | 2 | 7 | 6 | 9 | 3 | 8 |

## 4.16: What's missing?

At each step the entire image rotates 45° clockwise

## 4.17: Careful counting

There are 28 rectangles and squares in total

# Your progress notes

Use these pages to make notes on your progress.

Your Progress Notes

# *Track your points*

Each time you try a puzzle page, write a score in the POINTS box at the top of that page.

Give yourself 5 points if you tried a puzzle but could not complete it, or award yourself a full 10 points if you both tried *and* successfully completed a puzzle. For puzzles without specific solutions, such as creativity tasks, score 10 points for having a good attempt at it. Similarly, for memory tasks, give yourself 10 points if you feel you did your best at that task. Or, in both cases, 5 points for 'could try harder'.

Keep track of your chapter totals below, and then once you have worked through the entire book you can work out your overall points total:

**Chapter 1** [ ]

**Chapter 2** [ ]

**Chapter 3** [ ]

**Chapter 4** [ ]

**TOTAL** [ ]